Fit For Men

Fit For Men: A STUDY OF NEW YORK'S CLOTHING TRADE

By Egal Feldman

FOREWORD BY THOMAS C. COCHRAN

Public Affairs Press, Washington, D. C.

TO THE MEMORY OF
ARTHUR C. BINING

419 New Jersey Avenue, S.E., Washington 3, D. C.

Printed in the United States of America
Library of Congress Catalog Card No. 60-1550

FOREWORD

Beside the submerging of Victorian moral standards in sex, jazz, gin and general confusion, the nineteen-twenties marked the beginning of continuous study of business history. Some of the scholars were "new" social historians pursuing their duty of studying all aspects of American life, others were in schools of business, particularly Harvard, exploring the evolution of company administration. In the face of the difficulties of assembling adequate records the social historian's interest waned before it had waxed. Sparked by the determination of the late N. S. B. Gras, the interest of those at the Harvard Business School has been translated into more than a score of individual company histories, and scholars at other business schools have provided important additions.

In spite of at least fifty scholarly company histories and hundreds of others aimed at celebrating anniversaries or improving public relations, the early development of types of business, as a whole, in particular areas has been largely neglected. Occasionally some brief sketch of general business history finds its way into economic studies of industry, but good examples of the latter are scarce. Furthermore, marketing has been studied even less than production.

Lack of records has been a major barrier to study of the history of distribution or marketing. Prior to the Civil War the firms involved were always small, and like the annals of the poor, those of little business are short and simple. Small proprietors and partners kept important matters in their heads and saved space by throwing away old journals and ledgers. Men in the early years of the ready-made clothing business were not thinking of their place in history.

Egal Feldman has had, therefore, to rely upon such sources as travellers' accounts, city directories, almanacs, government reports and statistics, and periodicals to compensate for the lack of company records. Obviously he would have liked to know much more, but there were no promising clues to additional material. The historian has to make the best of what he has, which Mr. Feldman did.

Here is an interesting piece of the development of the great New York City market that came to dominate the United States. Those interested in the history of the city and its customs as well as business and economic historians will appreciate this little book.

THOMAS C. COCHRAN

University of Pennsylvania

PREFACE

This is an attempt to describe the growth of the New York clothing trade in its formative years.

As an opening date, 1800 has been chosen mostly for convenience; 1795 or even 1790 could have been selected just as well because no great economic change was visible in American economic life in either the last decade of the eighteenth century or the first few years of the nineteenth century. However, the year 1800, although it does not mark the starting point of any great historical movement, is a point that offers a contrast to the decades that followed. The year 1861 was chosen as a terminal date because it marks the end of an important chapter in the New York clothing trade.

The term "clothing trade" has been used in this study in its larger and broader sense. It includes not only buying, selling, and shipping at wholesale and retail in the United States, but also production and business organization, problems of technology, and labor. It is an all-encompassing term that is applied to every facet of both custom and ready-made clothing.

The word "clothing" in this study, however, is applied only to clothing for men, not including the boot, shoe, and hat industries, each of which would fill a volume in itself. This, then, is a survey of the production and sale of coats, vests, and trousers, and such furnishings as shirts, collars, and cuffs.

This study was undertaken with the encouragement of the late Arthur C. Bining. To his kindly criticism I owe a very great debt. I hope that the final product would have measured up to his expectations. Suggestions from Thomas C. Cochran of the University of Pennsylvania were of great help during the final stages of the study. I am also deeply grateful to the staffs of the New York Historical Society and the New York Public Library, whose unstinted patience and generous cooperation went beyond the call of duty on many occasions. Many thanks also to Mr. E. B. Ward and his advertising staff at Brooks Brothers, Inc. Mr. Ward not only permitted me to dig freely into the firm's dusty archives but also willingly contributed his own knowledge of the firm's past. Finally, editorial assistance was provided by Mrs. Jane Powell.

EGAL FELDMAN

New York City

CONTENTS

I

EARLY YEARS OF THE NINETEENTH CENTURY

Few signs of a clothing industry could be detected in Manhattan in the opening years of the nineteenth century. The handful of tailors whose shops sprinkled the lower tip of the island depended largely upon local transactions.

The manufacture of clothing was largely part of the housewife's routine chores in running her household. It was quite normal for her to lay out the wool or cotton fabric on the dining table, mark it, and with household shears or other sharp instruments cut out the article desired. As a result, there was little need to purchase ready-made clothing. If a more elegantly finished product was desired, an itinerant tailor was invited into the home to cut such items as suits for the men and boys. This tailor was often assisted in the sewing by a seamstress. Early nineteenth century newspapers carried many notices of families seeking seamstresses and seamstresses seeking families. Moreover, general house servants were expected to sew clothing, as well as to cook, clean, and wash.[1]

A government report in 1810 estimated that two-thirds of all garments worn by inhabitants of the United States were produced in the home. Even in the early 1820's much male apparel was cut on the dining table. In 1823 Amanda Jones prepared a manual on tailoring directed not at the professional tailor but at the housewife or her seamstress.[2]

Prices for apparel that was cut and made to order were very high. The custom tailor shops on lower Broadway and its adjoining thoroughfares were exclusive; their interiors were very seldom seen by the majority of the citizenry. Their shelves were piled high with imported plaids and cashmeres—luxuries beyond the reach of the average person.

Travelers were generally in agreement that it was more expensive to buy clothing in New York than in London. In 1817 one visitor claimed that garments were 25 to 100 per cent higher in price here than in England. Another complained of such high prices as $36 for a coat, $7 for a vest, and $10 for pantaloons. Isaac Holmes warned prospective immigrants to be prepared to pay heavily for clothing.[3] The account book of Henry S. Brooks, a Cherry Street merchant tailor, confirms the existence of high prices. In the summer of 1818 Brooks billed one customer $70 for a coat and pantaloons.[4] Other dealers charged prices equally as high. J. Burk, who had two clothing stores in Manhattan in 1822, asked $28 to $30 for a coat. In one of his advertisements, Burk conceded that "among the various necessaries of life, there is perhaps no article more expensive than the article of clothing." The American wool industry, yet in its infancy, and the custom tailor generally produced garments priced beyond the reach of the masses.

The high prices of woolen male apparel helped to increase the popularity of lower priced leather clothing. Pants, vests, and shirts were frequently made of leather.

In New York City in 1810 leather breeches could be procured in various fancy colors from B. Dyke, who also assured his patrons of "the most fashionable style." Some years later tailor Richard Yeo offered to clothe his customers "from head to foot" with leather shirts, drawers, waistcoats, and socks. Yeo, who considered his garments "health preservers, as they effectually protect the whole body from the most piercing winds and chilling winter's blast," conducted a leather clothing manufactory at 165 Water Street; he boasted numerous orders "from different parts of the Union."

II

EMERGENCE OF A CLOTHING CENTER

The limited sphere in which tailors operated lasted only a few years after the opening of the nineteenth century. It was not long before an abundance of clothing stores and tailor shops became a marked characteristic of growing New York. Visiting the city in 1805, Isaac Holmes warned prospective emigrant tailors not to come to New York, but to settle in rural areas and smaller villages.[1] New York City, he felt, was not the place for an enterprising tailor because there seemed to be too many tailors already.

The rapid multiplication of clothing stores is evidenced in city directories. One edition in 1805 listed 78 merchant tailors, 13 proprietors of clothing stores, and 3 clothiers. The clothing stores included a number of dealers in second-hand apparel; the majority of these dealers were found along the docks on Water, Pearl, and Front Streets. Others, not very far from Manhattan's tip, were on Chatham Square and the Bowery.[2] Longworth's directory for 1805 listed 188 tailors and tailoresses.[3] In 1816 Longworth listed 357 clothing entrepreneurs. The majority of these, 255, were called tailors. In addition, there were 40 merchant tailors, 40 tailoresses, 21 clothiers and proprietors of clothing stores, and 1 operator of a "slop shop."

By 1816 the city seemed to be well served by tailoring establishments, although the function of these outlets was mostly retailing to the local surrounding area rather than wholesaling to the south and west, a function soon to be assumed.

The exact date on which New York manufacturers began to produce for a national market is hard to determine. It probably occurred sometime between 1822 and 1830. In a review of the progress and origin of the wholesale clothing trade in the city, one writer remarked in 1864 that "this branch of industry . . . was almost unknown 40 years ago; the nearest approach to it in that day being the manufacture of clothing by a few individuals in this city who had branches for the sale of their goods at retail in some of the southern cities."[4]

In 1825, 378 tailors, 42 tailoresses, 50 merchant tailors, and 43 proprietors of clothing stores were listed in the city directory. Three years later the clothing industry employed about 2,000 people.[5]

By 1835 New York City had acquired the reputation of being the nation's leading center for the manufacture of ready-made clothing and a number of the larger firms were shipping clothing to all parts of the Union, as well as to foreign countries. A few firms were employing between 300 and 500 hands. Cornelius Baker and Co., Brewster and Co., William Gardner and Co., S. W. Moore and Co., Trask, Baldwin, and Lombard—all now forgotten—were leading wholesale houses in the city at that time.[6]

Unfortunately there are no statistics available to show the actual extent of the production of these early firms. The value of their products was undoubtedly small, compared with the output of later decades, but the growth of these companies in number is evidence of the unusually rapid rise of the city's clothing industry between 1822 and 1837.

The years 1837 to 1840 were bleak ones not only for the New York clothing industry but also for the American economy in general. Most of the firms mentioned above were dissolved during that time, never to be heard of again. Poised on a foundation of precarious and extensive credits, they were soon dragged down by defaulting storekeepers, particularly those in southern and western rural communities. By 1840, however, the trade began to revive and numerous new firms appeared. Moreover, the growing western market encouraged a greater production than ever before. In 1841 the value of clothing sold at wholesale in New York City was estimated at $2,500,000.[7]

Within the period 1840-1848 the manufacture of male apparel was said to have "increased more rapidly and extensively than the great increase of our commerce and population would seem to justify. . ." We are credibly informed, remarked an observer, "that New York supplies clothing for over two-thirds of the Union, the aggregate of the value of which is far greater than any other branch of manufacture in the city."

In this period other centers of manufacture were emerging and striving to share the national trade with the New York metropolis. For example, Cincinnati, strategically located to service the Old South and the New West, manufactured men's clothing valued at $1,940,450 in 1840. Ten years later Cincinnati's clothing trade was valued at $4,427,500, a 130% gain.[8] Nevertheless New York City maintained a distinct lead over its rapidly growing competitors.

By 1849 the larger New York houses were manufacturing enormous amounts of clothing. The general manager of Lewis and Hanford announced that during the winter of 1848-1849 his team of cutters cut

100,580 garments and that from November 1, 1848, to July 14, 1849, they cut an average of 1,135 garments per day."[9]

A survey of industries in New York State in 1850 showed that in terms of net value the manufacture of clothing was the third most important state manufacturing enterprise. Heading the list were the manufacture of metals, machines, and conveyances, with a total product value of $27,703,344, and the manufacture of wood products with a value estimated at $14,454,311. The clothing industry, which included millinery, was valued at $12,083,658. Such other industries as food, printing, building, textile, chemical, leather, and rubber trailed behind.[10]

The position of the New York clothing industry in 1850 can be even better appreciated by a comparison of the number of clothiers and tailors residing in that state with those residing in other states. In the seventh census, 3,780 clothiers and 52,069 tailors were enumerated in the entire United States. Of these, 454 clothiers and 12,692 tailors resided in New York. Of the remaining states, Ohio led in clothiers with 436 and Pennsylvania led in tailors with 8,787. Massachusetts had only 215 clothiers and 3,115 tailors and Connecticut counted just 79 and 673 respectively. Other figures are too small to be worth mentioning.[11]

The years 1850 to 1860 saw an even greater acceleration of the growth of the industry. For example, the value of clothing sold at wholesale in 1853 was estimated at nearly $20,000,000. That year a local business directory listed 410 clothiers engaged in both retailing and wholesaling, 85 clothiers specializing in wholesaling, 542 tailors, and 38 dealers in second-hand garments. In addition, in that survey, a relatively new element was included: the dealer in juvenile clothing. In the 1853 directory there were also 16 retail boys' clothing stores and 2 wholesale establishments.[12] In 1854 there were 444 combination retail-wholesale firms, 82 wholesale operations, 83 dealers in second-hand apparel, and 625 tailors.[13]

The New York State census of 1855 counted 126 tailor shops in the County of New York. These firms invested $1,068,550 in real estate and more than $50,000 in machinery, consumed raw materials valued at $4,317,302, manufactured garments valued at $7,592,696, and employed 12,968 workers. Separate estimates were listed for the clothiers, shirt and collar makers, and tailors. The County of New York included 403 clothiers, 267 shirt and collar makers, and 29,236 tailors.[14] In that year men's furnishings, by now a distinct field of business, produced goods valued at $601,000.[15]

By the mid-1850's the manufacture of men's clothing had assumed a solid place in the American economy. A fashion magazine estimated the annual investment in clothing in 1854 at nearly $500,000,000.[16] New York City, situated in a strategic position, had everything to gain by this enormous annual expenditure. In 1857, 106 New York clothiers dealt exclusively in wholesale operations. "It is well known," reported an observer in the summer of 1857, "that New York manufacturers now supply the greater quantity of clothing used throughout the States."

Toward the close of the decade New York manufacturers were both optimistic and confident of their place in the economy. "It will be apparent to everyone," stated the opening report of the New York State Chamber of Commerce in 1858, "that the increase of the clothing trade of New York must be continuous. Indeed the trade may be said to be but yet in its infancy; and what, with the increasing population of the country, the increasing facilities of reaching all points of it, and the centralization of this trade at New York, there is no telling the extent it may not reach." The report further stated that of the 130 leading firms in the city, 20 did business amounting "to fifteen millions per annum" and 20 others aggregated "five millions per annum. Of the other 90, there are a number who manufacture here for their establishments in the large cities of the South and West—some of them to the extent of two and three hundred thousand dollars."

By 1858 other cities shared with New York the task of supplying the increased national demand for ready-made clothing. Boston, for example, noted the "rapid development, and increasing importance" of its clothing trade and pointed out that "in 1840 there were only two houses who made any pretension to selling goods at wholesale, and their united business did not probably exceed $200,000 per annum." Fifteen years later that city boasted 30 wholesale ready-made clothing establishments with an annual production valued at $12,000,000.[17]

Although impressive, these figures do not approach those reported by New York City, which increased its wholesale business from $2,500,000 in 1841 to $20,000,000 in 1855. In 1858 a New York Chamber of Commerce report stated that "the wholesale clothing trade of New York is more than double the trade of Boston, Philadelphia, and Baltimore combined, and is every year drawing largely from the trade of these cities." Though it lacked precise statistical evidence, the report was fairly certain that business had increased during the previous 30 years at a rate faster than that of any other industry in the city. "One house alone," it declared, "gives employment to more hands at this moment, than were employed by all the houses in the wholesale clothing trade 30 years ago." That year, according to the report, about 32,000 people were employed by the clothiers and the annual retail and wholesale business totaled about $40,000,000.

In the midst of this amazing progress, the nation's clothiers were struck by the panic of 1857. This recession, first felt in 1856, was short but painful. The dark clouds on the horizon forced one writer to predict in 1856 that "the sales for the present year . . . will probably be less, not because the goods cannot be sold, but because prudent men think they discern in the times some signs that warn them to be cautious in extending credits." Of the 2,705 mercantile failures in the United States in 1856, 708 occurred in New York State. In New York City 915 stores failed between December 26, 1855, and December 25, 1857, and 406 additional firms failed in 1858.[18]

In their great haste to sell, New York clothiers kept their shops open late into the fall and winter nights of 1857 and slashed their prices mercilessly by 20, 40, and even 50 per cent. The retailers were the ones who suffered the most, because the wholesale clothing manufacturers, in their struggle to survive, declared war on their former customers and began to dispose of their stocks at retail at rock bottom prices. This short-circuit operation engendered "a deep and general feeling of indignation among retailers, who . . . [looked] . . . upon it as dishonorable" and complained that "wholesale houses are certainly formidable rivals to have to encounter at such a crisis, when they need all their energies to enable them to struggle through." Conceding that "to get money at any sacrifice is the object," the wholesalers felt forced to step "out of their ordinary line . . . [and sell] . . . their goods at three-fourths or two-thirds their value."

The clothing merchants, as did all the merchants at that time, reflected upon the causes that brought on the calamity. Why, they asked, did the long, fat years suddenly turn lean? J. J. Whiting, a member of the Boston Board of Trade and a close observer of the progress of the clothing industry, felt that one of the most important causes of the crisis was "the existing system of 'long credits.' I am quite sure," he declared, "that upon no class of businessmen does the long credit system bear more heavily than upon the wholesale clothiers. The credit usually allowed by them is much longer than is common by dealers in other goods, while a large proportion of their stock is paid for in actual cash to the persons employed in manufacturing." Now that the crisis had come, Whiting criticized the practice of wholesalers who in the rush for cash opened "their rooms to retail customers." He felt that that course was a cruel remedy that would only tend to prolong the crisis. Courting the consumer, he believed, would not compensate for the loss incurred by ruining the retailer. But he was confident "that a revival of business will take place early in the fall; and although the return of confidence may be slow, it will lead surely and progressively to prosperity."

The confident note struck at the close of Mr. Whiting's report did not prove to be a false one. By the end of August, 1858, a revival was noticed in the New York dry goods trade and in the following month vigorous activity was seen in the clothing houses. Moreover, western customers, who proved to be both the least reliable and the heaviest defaulters throughout the crisis, once again resumed payments. While clothiers noticed that collections from the West were "more satisfactory," they felt that it would "be a long time before they fully recover from their embarrassments." There was, however, a need for New York merchandise in the West, where a vacuum had been created during the critical period of light purchasing, and the stage was now set for a revival. By the spring of 1859 it was reported that "mechanical and other pursuits have started with renewed activity and vigor. Manufacturers are all busy . . . in fact, there seems to be full and profitable employment in New York for all who have any useful trade or calling."[19]

The setback of the short depression proved to be only a temporary one for the clothing houses. Recuperation was quick and progress was resumed almost instantaneously. In fact, the crisis taught the clothiers the need for both greater efficiency in production and more caution in business procedures. As a result, greater use was made of the sewing machine and numerous consolidations took place as small firms merged with larger ones. The census of 1860 showed an increase in production capacity but a decrease in the number of firms participating in the industry. "Many small shops," it reported, "have been merged into large wholesale establishments for the manufacture and sale of ready-made clothing." For the country as a whole, the census estimated an 11% drop in the number of firms and a 2.4% increase "in the aggregate number of hands employed." It added, however, that "the amount of capital invested in the business had augmented nearly 100%, and the aggregate value of the product 51.5%, as compared with the returns of 1850."[20]

In addition, the census showed that New York City not only continued to maintain its supremacy as a manufacturer of male apparel but also had increased its lead over all other urban areas. In 1860 in the United States there were 3,793 clothing establishments with a capital investment of $24,939,193, finished products valued at $73,219,-765, and 41,173 men and 57,730 women employees. Of these New York State had 860 establishments with a capital investment of $8,038,361, finished products valued at $25,095,299, and 14,767 men and 17,696 women employees. Further, more than half of the state's business was done in New York City.

No other area approached these figures. Pennsylvania, according to the census, was in second place with 672 establishments with a capital investment of $5,256,201, finished products valued at $12,305,541, and 7,828 men and 10,090 women employees. Massachusetts was in third place with 196 clothing firms with a capital of $1,498,400, finished products valued at $6,070,975, and 1,720 men and 3,927 women employees.[21]

The census contained a separate estimate of the production of men's shirts, collars, and furnishings that told a similar story. In the United States as a whole, it stated, 219 establishments were engaged in the production of men's shirts, collars, and furnishings. Their total capital investment amounted to $2,256,500 and they produced products valued at $7,218,790. Of these firms, 74—with a capital investment of $935,450 and a product valued at $3,779,111—were in New York State. Pennsylvania possessed more establishments than did New York—it had 81—but its capital investment was only $570,650 and its product was valued at only $1,359,614. In third place was Connecticut, which had 19 establishments with an invested capital of $547,000 and a product estimated at $1,322,900.

In the production of men's furnishings alone, New York made enormous strides between 1855 and 1860. The New York Chamber of Commerce estimated the increase between the state census of 1855 and the national census of 1860 at 27%. That percentage, however, was small when compared with the 124% increase in production of men's apparel in general.

Although the export trade in men's apparel was not the strongest factor in the growth of the early clothing trade, a study of its volume does reveal the strong position held by New York in this field. The figures for exports from ports of American cities between 1855 and 1860 show that out of all of the men's clothing manufactured in the United States between 1855 and 1856 goods valued at $278,832 were exported. That year New York City exported clothing valued at $183,148. In the following year $333,442 worth of clothing left all the ports of the Union and $161,636 worth left the port of New York City. During the recession of 1857 and 1858, clothing valued at $210,695 was exported from all ports and clothing worth $103,471 was exported from New York. In the following year total exports increased to $470,613, of which $156,028 was exported from New York. In the fiscal year from 1859 to 1860 national exports increased to $525,175 and New York City's share reached $215,606. No other American port—except, perhaps, San Francisco—could account for such a high percentage of the national exports of men's clothing. San Francisco exported clothing valued at $254,638 from 1858 to 1859 and $252,599 from 1859 to 1860.[22] However, most of the clothing that left San Francisco had been manufactured in New York City.

The New York clothing business had indeed made tremendous strides in the four decades preceding the Civil War. From a local, almost insignificant, industry, it had grown to a national leader. As a wholesale and retail center it had no peer. Its merchants, a confident and aspiring lot, began to look abroad for new fields to conquer and urged diplomats to pay less attention to negotiations with Latin American republics "for the right of way across continents, and the navigation of rivers" and more to the problem of "favorable tariffs to introduce and spread their manufactures." These merchants were on the lookout for "every country and island in the world, where there is a man to wear a coat." First and foremost, however, the growth of New York's clothing trade was due to its ability to capture the national market and to its emergence as a depot of national supply.

III

THE COUNTRY MERCHANT IN THE BIG TOWN

Early in the nineteenth century New York City became a favorite resort of country storekeepers who turned here to replenish their stocks of merchandise. The age of the traveling salesman—the man who represented the New York firm throughout the country—had not yet arrived and placing orders through a traveling salesman was a practice almost unknown in the United States before 1840 and not utilized very frequently prior to the Civil War. Since the merchant came to the salesman, rather than the salesman to the merchant, the number of storekeepers who arrived in the city served as a barometer of the business climate and was carefully watched by interested merchants.[1]

Twice each year streams of southern and western merchants flowed toward New York. They came in the spring "when the cold and winter season has disappeared, and given way to a warmer and more congenial climate" and in the fall before "the winter can reassert its influence, in closing up the varied channels of communication with the interior." Observing this movement, a traveler remarked in 1845 that "a stranger traveling at either of these seasons, on any of the great routes . . . from New York . . . would feel some surprise at meeting this immense concourse of people in such continued motion."[2]

Although the clothing buyers had at first turned to Philadelphia, Boston, and other cities to make their purchases, the New York clothing houses soon attracted them away from these cities and forced their attention here, where they could find "better and cheaper articles than they could manufacture or buy elsewhere." Numerous country merchants viewed the semi-annual trip to New York as an exciting interlude in their business affairs, but many others saw it as merely a tedious and expensive journey. Seldom was the trip undertaken for purchases amounting to less than $6,000, and a merchant coming to the city usually prepared himself for a trip of at least six weeks duration, four of which were usually devoted to traveling. Many merchants hoped that someday a system could be worked out whereby goods could be ordered "without the necessity of quitting . . . home for that purpose."[3]

There were, however, a number of storekeepers in the South and

West who managed to avoid the trip eastward. For example, the Andrews family, retailers of clothing in Huntsville, Alabama, in the late 1820's, stationed a partner in New York to make the purchases. In addition, a few western merchants in the 1840's purchased through companies that were set up for that very purpose. Others bought through agents and friends who lived closer to the seaboard. The majority, however, preferred to supervise their transactions personally and took the trip to New York themselves.

With the improvement of transportation in the 1850's some buyers increased the frequency of their trips to New York, "spread their purchases over a wider space and time" and used "more diligence and care in making selections."

Every effort was made by the clothiers to attract the storekeepers to the city. Then as now, advertising served as the principal means of bringing the consumers and producers together, and the New York newspapers, filled with advertisements of clothing merchants, circulated freely in the larger American towns. "A few days ago," announced a prominent metropolitan journal in the early spring of 1839, "we received an order . . . for 150 copies of the *Herald* to be sent regularly to New Orleans for one year." The same journal anticipated orders from other southern cities as well.[4]

The clothiers did not depend only on the circulation of New York newspapers throughout the country. They advertised extensively in the leading southern and western newspapers. In the summer of 1848 a column entitled "New York Advertisements" in the *New Orleans Daily Picayune* directed a series of convincing arguments toward the surrounding country merchants who might have some doubt about making purchases in New York. "There can be no doubt," it stated, "but that the City of New York is the most advantageous market in the United States for the purchase of country supplies." Outlining the reasons, it declared that the city "is connected by water communication and railroads with all the states . . . it receives the largest importations from abroad, contains the largest stocks of goods, and is the great depot of American manufactures; and prices are less, and credits more liberal."[5]

The clothing merchants devoted many lines of advertising to acquainting their distant potential customers of the natures of their stocks, the setups of their organizations, and the terms on which they did business. For example, F. J. Conant, one of the earliest and largest New York wholesalers, announced in a Savannah newspaper in 1831 that storekeepers coming to New York would find his place of business removed from its former location on Maiden Lane to 138 Pearl Street, where there was a stock of goods of "more extensive assortment than formerly" and where "the style, make and materials of the cloaks will be greatly improved and will be sold at about the same low prices as those of the last season." The stock of clothing, Conant added, consisted of a varying quality and style suitable for both the southern and western markets and "those who will take the trouble to examine the stock will probably satisfy themselves that they cannot select the same amount from any stock in the city that will be . . . safer or more desirable." He also assured the storekeepers that a liberal credit policy would be extended to them and that, if by chance they found the clothing unsalable, the stock would be readily "exchanged for others."[6]

A. and G. A. Arnoux, New York retailers of clothing, described their system of production for their southern customers thus: "There are three skillful artists employed in this establishment—one to cut coats, one to cut pants, and one to cut waistcoats. Each department is complete in itself . . . Strangers who visit this metropolis will find at this establishment everything to their taste."[7]

Naturally, most of the clothiers boasted that their garments were the best, that their fabrics were superior to all others, and that their prices were the most reasonable. The firm of Stilwell and Montross, which retailed in New Orleans and wholesaled in New York, announced that its garments "cannot be excelled in style and material." George P. Fox introduced himself to southern readers as a "cloth importer, leader of fashion and professed pantaloon maker" with twenty-one years of experience as a wholesaler and retailer. Wilde, Bates, and Taylor, manufacturers and wholesalers at 64 Nassau Street, claimed with little modesty that "their fall and winter stock . . . for extent, variety, style . . . cannot be excelled in the United States."

Dealers in men's shirts and furnishings, such as the proprietors of the New York wholesale shirt warehouse, also extended their invitations to country buyers. Another dealer, J. C. Lamphier, who boasted of his choice selection of "gentlemen's furnishing articles of the latest importation," printed his invitation in the "New York Advertisements" column of the *New Orleans Daily Picayune.*

Once in New York, the country storekeepers were again greeted with a multitude of requests for their patronage that appeared in the various local newspapers and city directories.

In 1824 J. T. Jacobs, proprietor of the United States Clothing Store at Maiden Lane and Nassau Street, urged southern and western merchants "to call and examine their stock of clothing, which will be sold on the lowest possible terms, by the case or package." F. J. Conant likewise offered persuasive arguments in the metropolitan journals. In the fall of 1834 he boasted " a very large stock of clothing, made in good style, of materials purchased out of season, much below their present value." R. L. Smith and Co. informed the merchants that it had on hand "1,200 men's cloaks, of various styles." Hobby, Husted and Co. announced in 1836 that "they will keep on hand a large supply of ready-made clothing of the best materials and workmanship, expressly calculated for the southern and western markets."[8]

The importance of the patronage of the southern and western country merchants can also be seen in the fact that when New York seamstresses and tailoresses were thrown out of work in 1837 they quickly organized the "Tailoresses and Seamstresses Clothing Establishment." One of this group's first steps was to request "southern and western orders for clothing" and to promise prompt execution "on the most moderate terms and in the best manner."[9] Even custom tailors did not overlook the presence of the country merchants. A few, such as William Pettit at 90 Fulton Street, continued their custom tailoring craft but prepared also to make up clothing "for the southern and western markets with neatness and dispatch."

The manufacturers of shirts and men's furnishings also found the presence of the country storekeepers in their midst an encouragement to advertise. John Clay wrote of his "magnificent and elegantly finished assortment of striped shirts well adopted to the southern market." Palmer and Farr of 476 Broadway announced that orders for their "fine linen shirts" may be "executed for any part of the country." John Woolsey, who operated a "wholesale shirt warehouse," invited "southern and western merchants . . . to call" and to examine the "large assortment of shirts of every quality made in the latest styles, and of superior workmanship."

One of the leading clothing houses of the 1850's was D. and J. Devlin, which constantly invited "western and southern merchants to call and look." Its stock, it declared in 1851, "will be found greater in extent and variety than has ever been got up by any house in the trade." At the commencement of the appropriate season it notified jobbers and merchants from the South and West that its "stock of spring and summer wear" or its "fall and winter stock" was ready for sale. It was also noted that "the wholesale customers of Messrs. Devlin and Co. come from every point. They supply the North, South, East, and West, each with the peculiar kind of goods required by them."

A commercial observer wrote that it was difficult to "estimate the advantages to the commerce of our city of such houses as Devlin and Co. Their success and the popularity of their manufacture have contributed . . . more than any other cause within our knowledge to draw to New York vast numbers of customers from all parts of the Union to make their purchases . . . exclusively in New York. This fact alone is sufficient to place the clothing trade of our city in the front rank in point of commercial importance."

Once the country storekeepers arrived in the city, there was a mad rush to win their patronage, and newspaper advertisements filled with notices of competing firms could not alone be relied upon to guarantee sales. The clothing manufacturers had made up their stocks in advance; the raw materials, in many cases, had been purchased on credit; and their numerous employees had to be paid in cash. As a result, if a sale could not be closed in a hurry, conditions could become catastrophic. Therefore there was a rush to ferret out the storekeepers from hotel lobbies and rooms and, if necessary, neighboring cities.

There was little difficulty in finding the merchants once they arrived in the city. They were conspicuous in the lobbies of all of the major hotels and their names were registered in a book open to the public for examination.[10] Mercantile agents known popularly as "drummers" or "runners" circulated in the hotel lobbies, checked the credit ratings of the new arrivals, and got quickly to work. "This duty," wrote one traveler, "is generally intrusted to young men of some talent, genteel appearance . . . who in the business seasons, reside . . . as boarders at some one of these hotels. They are ever watchful and attentive to their calling." They had to be clever, since their salaries depended upon the sales they could make. And since they usually received 2½ per cent, they were also dubbed "two-and-a-half-per-cent salesmen." Moreover, they were extremely persistent at times.

One story is told of a Mr. Pike who was sent from New York to Philadelphia for the sole purpose of inducing a country storekeeper of good credit to return to the city with him and to place orders with a New York firm. Pike succeeded marvelously. He got Nap, the country merchant, to New York and did not let him out of his sight until he ran up a bill for $30,000, quite a haul indeed. But Pike was in no mood to rest: "other victims demanded . . . attention. This one has been put through; and they had no further use for him until his bills should mature."[11] Although this tale may contain more fiction that truth, it aptly suggests a condition that was generally prevalent.

It is not surprising, therefore, that after a while this method of pursuing the country merchants began to fall into disrepute. In fact, one clothing firm, P. L. Rogers and Co., emphasized in its advertisements "that it has repudiated the 'runner' method of getting customers." It warned visitors to be on the lookout for such agents whom, it felt, were only attached to disreputable houses.[12]

Furthermore, by the eve of the Civil War, the "drummer" himself was undergoing a complete transformation. He was gradually being converted into a traveling salesman and sent into the interior to make the acquaintance of the country merchants. Only when he had established a sufficient patronage in the rural areas was he invited to take his place in the front office at home.[13]

The New York Clothier and the Credit System. An outstanding factor in the attraction of the country merchants to New York was the liberal credit policy offered by the metropolitan tailors. The clothing merchants entered into few transactions on a cash basis. To have demanded cash would have been futile, since the country merchants commanded nearly none of it at the time of purchase: they, too, transacted business on good faith. Thus, a chain of credit extended from the New York merchants to the country storekeepers and thence to the rural consumers. If crops were good, crops and cash streamed backwards. The entire credit process took anywhere from six to eighteen months or longer. Usually, no interest was charged for the first six months, and interest for longer periods ranged up to about 10 per cent. Considering the risk involved in the event of a crop failure, this was indeed a liberal policy. Since no similar facilities to make huge purchases on a credit basis were open to the southern and western storekeepers at home, it is not surprising that they turned to New York to make their purchases.[14]

The very lifeline of the New York clothing trade consisted of a chain of credits, since that system was employed in both wholesale and local retail transactions. Even the most fashionable New York tailors conducted business largely on a credit basis. As a result, many people complained that the tailors, in order to protect themselves against the bad risks that they frequently took, overcharged on each garment as an "insurance on each item," and thus made "the honest pay the losses occasioned by the dishonest."[15]

As the period progressed and the clothiers experienced two severe panics and depressions—in 1837 and 1857, respectively—there was a tendency, at least among the retailers, to attempt to conduct business on a cash basis. The wholesalers, however, because they depended upon transactions with the South and West, were forced to maintain a credit policy and to wait at times from six months to two years for payments.

A number of wholesalers announced their credit terms in newspaper advertisements. For example, in 1831 F. J. Conant announced that his terms were " 6 months for approved notes payable at banks in good standing in any part of the country—8 months for city acceptances or 5 per cent discount for cash. In all cases when time is extended, interest will be charged at the rate of 6 per cent per annum."[16]

In 1836 the clothing firm of Young and Van Eps, which disappeared during the panic of 1837, informed its southern customers of its credit terms and declared an allowance of "6 months, for notes payable at banks of good standing in any part of the Union. In all cases where the time is extended," however, it said, "interest will be charged at the rate of 7 per cent per annum" and "a deduction of 2½ per cent will be made on city acceptances."

Following the panic of 1837 there was a strong attempt by a number of clothiers to conduct their business on a cash basis. Alfred F. James, who dealt with southern and western merchants, declared that his "terms must be cash" and called his place of business the "cash tailoring establishment." Many others described themselves by the same term at this time, but it is doubtful whether any of them were successful. As the years turned prosperous, most of the clothiers became glued to a policy of extending "every facility . . . to time buyers."

Toward the end of the period the credit structure proved to be a heavy burden to the small producer who was not in a position to command substantial capital to tide him over the long waiting period. "I am quite sure," wrote one observer, "that upon no class of businessmen does the long credit system bear more heavily than upon the wholesale clothiers." Production of the garments began about four months before the arrival of the country storekeepers. If a sale was consummated, a period of at least six months ensued before a clothier would receive his return. It was generally recognized by the late 1850's "that a large capital is necessary to carry on an extensive [clothing] business."[17] The mergers and consolidations of a number of firms in those years were no doubt partly due to the burden of the credit system.

Since business transacted on a credit basis was a procedure loaded with risks, it demanded that the clothier move cautiously to survive. Therefore, meeting the country merchant face to face was of the utmost importance in order to engineer business. As a result, the agents of mercantile firms who were lodged in the New York hotels were there not only to sell but also to see if the prospective customer was able "to 'pass muster'; that is, considered of sufficient solvency." If he was, then he was "immediately waited upon by a numerous bevy of agents."

Before business was transacted between a wholesaler and a storekeeper, a written application for credit was signed by the latter. Such a statement set "forth specifically the amount of his assets and liabilities . . . together with such other particulars as may be thought necessary to enable the giver of the credit to pass upon the responsibility of the applicant." In addition, the applicant for credit, if unknown to the wholesaler, was expected to have a letter of "introduction and credit" from one of the reliable customers of the wholesalers. This letter introduced the new customer to the wholesaler and vouched for his integrity.[18]

Many of the New York wholesalers kept a careful check on their customers' business activities. For example, the firm of Fisher, Blashfield, and Co., dealer in men's shirts and dry goods, kept the following notes on its western customers:

"Michigan: J. J. Mead, Farmington, Oakland Co. Worth $2,000—Doing fair bus. Good standing–making money.

"Illinois: James Sully, Canton, Fulton Co. Does a fair bus.—seems to be making money—has some Capl—good bus. character—may be worthy of credit.

"Indiana: Thomas F. Purnell, Indianapolis, Marion Co. Bred to business—married a young lady worth 4 m cash & 2 m in goods—Entirely safe & of good character.

"Missouri: A. F. W. Webb & Co. Hard pushed–may fail—seem to be trifling with their credit.

"Ohio: M. S. & J. Rusy, Navarre Starke Co. Are young—of fair promise—have no capt. of their own—friends probably help them. . .

"Wisconsin: Wm. Hall & Co. Milwaukie. H. is fond of horse-racing—keeps a horse—does not attend to business as he ought—lives beyond his means . . . doubtful credit . . . would not trust him."

Similarly keen observations were made of the firm's southern customers:

"North Carolina: A. Mickle & Co. Hillsboro, Orange Co. of high moral standing–M especially . . . both were worth probably enough to make them good for all they will buy.

"South Carolina: Wm. Howland, Charleston . . . formerly H. & Caskin & failed . . . *debts turning out . . . very good anyway.*

"Louisiana: Reuban Drake . . . has the reputation of being very rich

—much talked of as a speculator . . . no doubt is very strong though somewhat extended."[19]

After the panic of 1837 the wholesale merchants formed a Merchants Vigilance Association whose task it was to pry into the credit standings of storekeepers throughout the United States. Its chief investigator, Sheldon P. Church, began his career in 1827. He traveled extensively throughout the South and West and submitted weekly reports concerning the business standings of the many merchants he visited to the New York group.

In 1841 the first credit agency was formed by Lewis Tappan. It was called the Mercantile Agency. This firm gradually accumulated a mass of information concerning buyers throughout the country. In 1859, when Robert G. Dun emerged as its sole proprietor, the agency changed its name to R. G. Dun and Co. Today it is known as Dun and Bradstreet.

Although some clothing houses, such as C. T. Longstreet and Co., claimed to "rely more upon the character of the man who applies for credit and his statements than upon the reports obtained from mercantile agencies, or other sources of information," most clothiers no doubt took a keen interest in the agency's credit reports.

New York City as a Center of Importation of Ready-Made Clothing. In this period the city had also emerged supreme as an import center of ready-made clothing, and this factor helped to sway the country merchants to come here for their purchases. Where else could they choose from such a bewildering variety of imports?

Early in the century visitors to the city observed that huge quantities of fashionable ready-made clothing were imported into the metropolis from both France and England. In January, 1818, New York City shippers inaugurated a regular sailing schedule between the city and Liverpool. The result of this innovation was to mar the city from the start as an important western terminal for European imports.[20]

Recognizing the handwriting on the wall a number of New York tailors dropped their needles and turned to importing ready-made apparel for men. Among the first of these tailors was English-born James Chesterman, who arrived in the city "quite poor" from Lancashire in about 1800 and shortly afterward opened a tailoring shop in the vicinity of John and Nassau streets. During the 1820's he turned to the importation of ready-made clothing. Chesterman was soon reputed to be one of the wealthiest men in the city: his fortune grew from $200,000 in 1842 to $1,000,000 in 1855.[21]

The importers of ready-made clothing received their foreign goods packed tightly in "cases" or "camphor wood trunks" and then proceeded to dispose of them by advertising. "To southern and western merchants" Jas. McCarthy Murphy announced in 1833 that he had just received "an extensive assortment of summer garments . . . made up in Europe in the best style and of the best material."

The clothing manufacturers quite naturally viewed the importers as deadly rivals. Flooding the market with "slops" from the Old World, they said, was no way to stimulate a domestic clothing industry. Just the same, few of them approved of the protective measures that were enacted to raise the duties on imported ready-made clothing from 30% ad valorem in 1816 to 50% in 1828. They argued that since these duties pertained also to woolen textiles they tended to do more harm than good. Charles Cox, a New York tailor, referred to the 50% duty as "the accursed tariff." One objector argued that because of the tariff a London agent was successfully traversing the country "procuring orders for London-made clothes" and taking advantage of our preference "for everything, of English origin." This objector added that "under the present rates of duty on cloth & clothing, a suit of clothes can be regularly imported at a less price than one of the same quality would cost if made up in this country," and warned that "before long some of our most dashing and fashionable merchant tailors will . . . find their custom woefully fallen off." Such complaints were confirmed by an English visitor who "was told at New York of a person going into Canada to furnish his winter wardrobe, and finding, on his return . . . that the difference of prices between the two countries just covered his traveling expenses going and returning."[22]

The New York clothier, however, probably realized that heavy clothing importations would only tend to strengthen the general advantages of the city's clothing market, and by the 1850's no port in the United States could compare with the city in the volume of importations of ready-made garments. In the fiscal year from 1855 to 1856, for example, ready-made clothing valued at $404,133 was imported into the combined ports of the United States, and New York City's share was valued at $177,159. In the following year total United States imports added up to $347,471, nearly half of which—$142,038— entered at New York City. From 1857 to 1858 total imports were valued at $322,024, and the city's share was valued at $88,990. In the following year the city received clothing valued at $94,030 out of a national total of $284,849. From 1859 to 1860 the city's share of garments valued at a total of $346,059 was $123,332.

Two other cities, New Orleans and San Francisco, shared the

leadership in importations with New York. In fact, for two years, San Francisco maintained a slight edge over New York City: it imported clothing valued at $121,933 from 1857 to 1858 and at $101,-105 from 1858 to 1859.[23] But these markets were not in competition with New York; rather, they were extensions of the city's distribution facilities, and sales of ready-made clothing in New Orleans and San Francisco meant greater profits for the New York clothing merchant.

The chief sources of ready-made apparel from abroad were England and France which, respectively, supplied clothing valued at $153,178 and $155,845 from 1855 to 1856, $78,351 and $168,624 from 1856 to 1857, $76,498 and $145,383 from 1857 to 1858, $90,148 and $119,044 from 1858 to 1859, and $84,255 and $175,056 from 1859 to 1860.

New York as a Center of Textile Importations. The very factors that made the city a center of importation of ready-made clothing also made it a chief receiving depot of European textiles. This not only gave the manufacturers an advantage over rival producers in other urban areas but also tended to increase the attractiveness of the New York clothing market for the country purchaser.

In the years before 1860 American textile production was in no position to compete with the product available from European sources, chief of which were England and France. The English textile mills were greatly dependent upon American purchases: 40% of their exports of woolen fabrics entered American ports in 1799 and 30% in 1851. Although by the end of the 1850's American textile producers were able to supply the native clothiers with a good portion of the cheaper fabrics, they were in no position to compete with the foreign sources of better-grade textiles. By 1858 "broadcloth and other fine fabric" were said to be "entirely supplied from Europe." That year the New York Chamber of Commerce reported "that American wool, when used alone, cannot produce cloth of equal quality and finish as that made of foreign wools" and estimated that more than half of the expenditures on fabrics made by the city's clothing manufacturers went for foreign products.[24]

The popularity of textiles from abroad played directly into the hands of the New York clothier. Dealers in woolens, worsted goods, fancy goods, linens, silks, cashmeres, and vestings dotted the streets of lower Manhattan and were ready to serve the tailor in all his needs. Moreover, in the 1840's and later, when the New England mills increased their textile production, their product, too, was shuttled to New York. As a result, the city's clothing merchants were able to lay their hands on the raw materials first and, thereby, to offer the most rapid service to the visiting buyers.

Country merchants at times took advantage of the New York facilities for procuring raw materials: a number of them purchased their fabrics separately and then turned them over to the clothing manufacturers, who completed the fabrication. Mann and McKimm, clothing manufacturers since 1832 at 25 Carmine Street, specialized, according to their advertisements, in such a service. In the spring of 1844 they informed merchants who wished to have their own goods manufactured that "they are prepared to manufacture any description of clothing."

Generally, however, it was the clothier himself who procured the raw materials, by any one of a number of channels.

If he was a small producer, he could turn to the numerous auction sales which disposed daily of foreign and domestic dry goods in the lower part of the city. Walking along Pearl Street in 1832, a visitor noticed that "every corner presented an auction of some kind or other." Purchasing dry goods at auction remained an important procedure throughout this period. "No retailer," claimed a merchant with years of experience, "whose business is of any extent, can expect to cope with the competition he will inevitably meet, who does not to some extent adopt this plan of purchasing." He warned, however, that "like many other things, it may be done to excess," since goods of the highest quality were scarce at auction disposals.[25] It has, in fact, been suggested that auction sales helped to condition the American consumers to wearing garments of cheaper fabrics.[26] Many clothiers who took advantage of the auction sales proudly announced the fact in their advertisements and claimed that because of such purchases they were able to pass substantial savings on to their customers.

Another road open to the clothing manufacturer was that of purchasing the raw materials from the importer or jobber. This was no problem, since there were countless such middlemen throughout the business area of the city; and their advertisements, which filled the newspapers from 1800 to 1860, competed for the patronage of the custom tailors and wholesalers. "Fashionable waistcoating of various descriptions . . . black and colored collar velvets" and "superfine cloths and cashmeres suitable for merchant tailors" were announced in advertisements early in the century. Most of the middlemen were found in the Pearl Street area, almost next door to each other and the clothiers. Prior to 1830 many such dealers were the agents of British manufacturers. Later the goods were handled largely by the American merchants and importers themselves.

To serve their customers better a number of importers in the 1850's stocked their shelves with "buttons, cords, braids, bindings, threads, twist, sewing silk, etc., etc.," and numerous other paraphernalia important to the clothier. For example, the firm of Wilson G. Hunt offered manufacturers of clothing in 1853 a "complete stock of cloths," as well as "linings, trimmings, etc."[27]

By the mid-1850's supplying the tailor with trimmings became a profitable pursuit in itself. It was remarked in the fall of 1855 that the trimming houses of New York "were never so well supplied either in richness of variety or quality." E. W. Tryon and Co. and Thomas N. Dale and Co. "were the first to commence catering for the trade by rich selections from abroad." And it is not surprising to learn that a number of the leading trimming merchants had broken away from "cloth importation houses" after many years in that broader line.

Thus, the clothing merchants were surrounded by many who were eager to serve them and, by the 1850's, importers and jobbers of domestic and foreign cloth and trimmings competed for their favor at their very doorsteps.

As the period progressed, numerous clothing houses began to import their own fabrics or to contract directly with American textile manufacturers, thereby eliminating the middlemen and the expense of their services.

Moreover, supplementary dealings in men's dry goods and trimmings were practiced by the clothiers themselves even early in the century. Robert Cocks, a merchant tailor, sold in 1807 "best superfine cloths, French and Dutch blacks, blues and browns of superior quality . . . with a fresh supply of American buttons." A few years later it was noticed that a number of tailors kept "rather large stocks of woolen piece goods" on hand. The first account book of the Brooks clothing firm shows that sales consisted not only of clothing but also of "12 yards cashmere" and "2 dozen buttons." The firm of William Mitchell and Co. was wholesaling "elegant Valentia, Marseilles and rich silk Florentine vestings," as well as "superior London cloths and cashmeres," in addition to offering its service of custom tailoring. The "Cash Tailoring Establishment" of James and Taylor was also listed in 1838 as dealers in "cloths, cashmeres, vestings, and tailors' trimmings."[28] The firm of John Hazard Browning, predecessor of today's Browning King and Co., squeezed out the jobber and importer early in its career. In 1823 Browning contracted directly with C. A. Whitman, manufacturer of woolen goods, for a supply of plaids. Browning continued his dealings with Whitman in the following years.[29]

After 1840 many of the New York clothing houses imported their raw materials directly from abroad. The proprietors or senior or junior partners of various firms traveled abroad, visited foreign manufacturers, and established connections with the leading European cloth houses, thereby completely eliminating the need for the services performed by the dry goods jobber. In 1842 one firm announced that it possessed "the advantage of being connected with an extensive cloth establishment in Europe." Another declared that it could sell clothing at a lower price, since its cloth was purchased "from first hands." The large Chatham Street dealer, George T. Green, claimed in 1844 to have "made arrangements to receive cloths, cashmeres, vestings . . . by every packet." The firm of H. and D. H. Brooks and Co., later known as Brooks Brothers, claimed to import all its cloth from abroad. Likewise, the large wholesale house of Daniel and J. Devlin declared in 1851 that "one of the firm now visits periodically the European markets," seeking there "all the latest and best styles of goods."

In the 1840's and 1850's a number of clothing firms enlarged their organizations by combining with dry goods and trimming houses, thus furthering the trend to eliminate the services of the dry goods jobber and importer. The firm of Charles Cox declared in 1843 that it "has removed to 33 Maiden Lane . . . in connection with Galley & Rising's cloth and trimming store." In 1851 Tweedy, Moulton, and Plimpton, importers and jobbers of dry goods, were found united with William Gardner, a dealer in ready-made clothing. Their place of business at 47 Broadway was said to be so arranged that "in the upper stories" was found "a complete and general assortment of ready-made clothing" and in its lower a "full and general assortment of staple and fancy, domestic and foreign dry goods." The firm of Jesse Seligman—he was later prominent as a New York banker—was listed on the eve of the Civil War as a partnership between himself and his brothers, Joseph, James, and William, who were both importers of dry goods and wholesale clothiers.[30]

By 1857 the men's clothing industry had attained an almost "undisputed monopoly" in the handling of dry goods for men's wear. This trend was clearly noticed in a survey of American manufacture of 1860 which stated that the growth of the clothing industry "has wrought an important change in the dry goods trade. The importation and sale of foreign and domestic cloths has fallen, in a measure, into the hands of wholesale clothing merchants, who thus unite the jobbing business with that of manufacturers and dealers in clothing on a large scale."[31]

By the close of the period any change in the demand for wool fabrics by the clothing houses caused serious repercussions in the wool trade. For example, when the ready-made clothing industry began to demand a cheaper fabric in the 1850's, the high-quality British woolen manufacturers were seriously hurt. Likewise, spare buying by the clothing houses in the spring of 1860 proved to be painful to the foreign fabric houses.

Clothing Auctions in New York. The popularity of the New York auctions proved to be another source of attraction to the country buyers. It was felt that the lower prices that prevailed at these sales were the compelling factors that drew the storekeepers. One visitor to New York believed that the same goods at auction were at times priced 75 per cent lower than in retail stores.[32]

Other cities, too, had auction sales, but in none were the auctions regulated as they were in New York. The auction law of 1817 provided that goods once presented must be offered to the highest bidder and not be withdrawn. In other cities such a regulation did not prevail and the highest bidder was never assured of his purchase. Other regulations in New York provided that auctions be held during specified daytime hours and "that the conditions of sales be reduced to writing, printed, and publicly announced, prior to the commencement of the sale." The name of the auctioneer and the goods to be auctioned were also to be previously announced "in one or more of the city newspapers." These regulations gave the system an air of regularity and legitimacy, although visitors were warned to beware of "mock auctions" operating on side streets, beyond the pale of the law.[33]

In the early years of the century auctions were largely devoted to the disposal of foreign textiles dumped in American ports. But, as American manufactures began to grow, the auctions proved to be a popular outlet for these products, also.

Disposing of goods at auction had certain advantages to the growing American manufacturers. At an auction, an elaborate sales organization was not needed. And an auction was a good place to feel out and test demand and prices and to dispose of second-hand, damaged, and out-of-season stock. In fact, a strong argument against the auctions was that they tended to throw upon the market a cheaper-grade commodity that a respectable firm would not handle.[34] Obviously, the auctions were well suited for the sale of cheap ready-made clothing of either foreign or domestic origin.

It was quite clear that the southern and western merchants were the primary targets of the clothing auctioneers. When Samuel Whitmarsh, tailor and manufacturer of ready-made clothing, decided to throw "an extensive assortment of summer garments" into an auction sale in April, 1833, he called "to southern and western merchants." He had originally prepared the lot of garments for city retailers but, for some reason, had failed to unload it and had decided to dispose of it at auction. Similarly, J. T. Doughty announced that year a public auction of "500 lots ready-made clothing comprising a choice assortment suitable for . . . southern trade."[35]

All auctions of ready-made clothing were announced in advance and each announcement specified the time and place of the auction and gave a brief description of the merchandise to be auctioned. R. N. Harrison and A. Levy announced on April 27, 1833, that on April 30, 1833, "at 10 o'clock, a quantity of clothing, for the season, consisting of frock and dress coats, pantaloons, vests . . . " would be hammered off. John Sniffen of 217 Pearl Street announced in advance that on Saturday, April 26, 1834, "at 10 o'clock . . . the stock of a clothing store, consisting of coats, pantaloons, roundabouts, vests, trowsers," would be auctioned. Henry E. Riell declared in 1842 that his stock of "new and second-hand clothing" was "ready for examination, with catalogues."

The auctioneers did not deal exclusively with ready-made clothing. A few merely devoted one or two afternoons or mornings each week to that field. At other times they auctioned anything from furniture to watches, because they were, after all, in the auction, not the clothing, business. It is interesting to note that some did devote a considerable amount of time to the sale of men's clothing and were sometimes referred to as "clothing auctioneers." Thomas Bell was an example of this group. His career as an auctioneer, which was long and probably successful, stretched from the late 1830's to the mid-1850's. He started at 72 Chatham Street, but soon gave up that store and, in 1839, opened two new salesrooms—one at 32 Ann Street and the other at 115 Fulton Street. In 1840 he closed his Ann Street store and opened one at 22 John Street. Bell was one of the first auctioneers to announce auctions of boys' and children's clothing, as well as men's.

By the close of the 1850's the auctions served not only as outlets for rejected garments manufactured in and around the metropolis but also —if descriptions in their announcements can be relied upon—as places to buy clothing of superior quality, such as "cashmere, doeskin and satinet pants; silk . . . and velvet vests."

New York City as a Center for Second-Hand Clothing. As a center for the distribution of second-hand men's apparel, Chatham Street had a national reputation in the years preceding the Civil War. Although the census report of 1860 tried to tone down the fact that here people were "compelled to wear the castoff clothing of another, as in countries where the poor are more numerous," city directories and newspaper advertisements showed that even at that late date the trade in discarded garments was booming. The New York business directories show that 38 dealers in second-hand clothing were listed for 1854, 83 for 1855, 54 for 1857, and 100 for 1863. Pawnbrokers, too, were dealers in second-hand clothing, and it is interesting to note that they were most numerous in New York. Of the 72 pawnbrokers in the United States in 1850, 45 were in New York, 19 in Pennsylvania, and 6 in New Jersey.

A number of dealers in second-hand clothing—such as H. Levett, John K. Murray, and Thomas D. Conroy—clearly stated in their requests for discarded garments that they were seeking such apparel in order to fill orders for southern and western portions of the United States. Levett, who was active in the second-hand clothing business throughout the 1830's and 1840's, offered liberal sums for discarded garments in 1839 because he had "effected arrangements with his correspondence of the western country, for the transportation of castoff clothing." Murray announced in the winter of 1856 that he was in need of "$10,000 worth of new and castoff clothing . . . for city and western markets." Several years later, Conroy, located at 46 Centre Street, requested "any quantity of gentlemen's left-off clothing . . . for which fifty per cent more than their supposed value will be paid by calling at the store." One merchant, who signed himself "E. H.," sounded almost desperate in 1861 when he announced "a large order received—$8,000 worth of castoff clothing to purchase within one month, for the California market."[36]

A study of advertisements shows that the big problem faced by the second-hand dealer was not unloading his stock—there seems to have been plenty of opportunity for that–but purchasing it. Requests to sellers always assumed a more prominent portion of the advertisements than did requests for buyers, and numerous inducements were used to convince the city's dandies to clear their wardrobes of the past season's styles.

The Chatham Street dealers, M. Lumley and Morrison and Levy, appealed to the benevolent side of their patrons. "Gentlemen hitherto not having been in the habit of selling their castoff clothing," wrote Lumley, "will reflect that they can give the proceeds in charity, a system adopted by many gentlemen with whom the subscriber deals."

Morrison and Levy pointed out that "discarded clothing are frequently put aside as useless during the summer and destroyed by moths, while the produce of the sale might be appropriated to benevolent purposes, and the mechanic be enabled to appear respectable at prices within his means." All stressed the "very liberal prices" or the "highest cash price" offered. I. M. Dusseldorp advised those about to leave the city to sell their old clothing and to travel light. In addition, dandies were always reminded of changing fashions and the uselessness of last season's dress. A number of second-hand dealers stressed the point that a trip to Chatham Street was unnecessary: "a line per post," they said, was all that was really required, because they would be glad to pick up the garments themselves.

Not all of the apparel stocked by the dealer was second-hand. Cheap and faulty ready-made clothing and garments damaged by either fire or water were also picked up wholesale at auction or at special sales. Once procured, these garments were washed and renovated and sold as new.[37]

The chief attraction of this type of merchandise to the buyer was, of course, the price. In an age when the prices for men's apparel were relatively high, it is not surprising that second-hand clothing was purchased to a large extent. One authority went as far as to state that in the years "prior to the Civil War, the trade in second-hand clothing was perhaps more important than that in ready-made." Although former wholesale prices seem to be unavailable now, some idea of the inexpensiveness of second-hand, damaged, and discarded clothing can be gained from the retail prices that were occasionally listed. In 1849 dress coats were available for as low as $2, pants for $1, fancy silk and linen vests for 50 cents. Second-hand dealers, such as George Levie in 1849, were among the first to feature a complete "suit" of pants, vest, and coat for $5.[38]

Authough profitable, the trade in second-hand clothing was not considered a very attractive pursuit. Its control was largely in the hands of newcomers to New York—the Jews and, if names can be relied upon, the Irish. An observer from the South commented in 1851 that the clothing district in Chatham Street "is sometimes called Jerusalem, from the fact that the Jews do most, if not all, the business on this street" with "a Yankee stuck in now and then by way of variety."[39] Indeed, most contemporary comments of pre-Civil War Chatham Street bulge with contempt and ridicule and display little insight into the economic function of the trade. For example, George G. Foster, in *New York in Slices*, published in 1849, had this to say: "Step into the nearest clothing store in Chatham-Street and slip on a coat—*any* coat—and we'll wager our wedding-suit that it is a 'splendid fit.' There is no such thing as an ill-fitting coat in Chatham Street. Every coat there fits everybody."[40]

Along Chatham Street, Foster noticed that "clothing stores line the southern sidewalk, without interruption; and the coat-tails and pantaloons flop about the face of the pedestrian, like the low branches in a wood path. In front of each, from sunrise to sundown, stands the natty, blackbearded and fiercely-moustached proprietor; every now and then venturing, when a countryman passes, to tap him delicately on the arm, and invite him to look at the 'magnificent assortment' of wares and wearables within. Stooping, as you enter the low, dark doorway, you find yourself in the midst of a primitive formation of rags, carefully classified into vests, coats and pantaloons."

Foster also warned country visitors of "the expertness acquired by the keepers of these shops in 'spotting' their man . . . they know a greenhorn from the country by instinct; and there is something almost beautiful in the certainty with which they pounce upon him and the tenacity with which they cling to him. No matter what he wants, or whether he wants anything—they are sure to fit him. If he won't buy new clothes, they will sell him old ones . . . and . . . send him off fully impressed with the idea that he is not only the best dressed but the best-looking man in the city. If his toggery, however, holds together till he gets home, he may account himself a fortunate individual."

Before leaving for New York, southerners were also warned at times of the bad habit of purchasing from Chatham Street dealers. "Such habits break out on you more and more every day," cautioned a New Orleans newspaper, "and you can expect nothing less than being eventually regularly sewed up."

Such comments make good satirical reading but offer little illumination in regard to the commercial function of the second-hand clothing trade. As a means of offering young America an opportunity to dress comfortably yet inexpensively in an age when ready-made clothing was scarce, the trade in second-hand apparel had its place. One study went as far–perhaps too far—as to state that "the manufacture of ready-made clothing was probably an outgrowth of the second-hand clothing business" and that "the second-hand clothing business had established markets and trade customs that were taken over by the ready-made clothing manufacturers."[41]

Dealers in second-hand clothing were also important in another sense. They were among the first to establish the clothes-cleaning business on a commercial basis. Since the cleaning and repairing of clothing were important preliminaries in their task, it is not surprising that they became experts in these operations and that it was not long before they began accepting separate orders for cleaning and repairing. Many of these dealers included in their requests for discarded clothing statements of their willingness to accept orders for cleaning and repairing. Thomas L. Jennings announced in 1828 that he "also scours and repairs in the neatest manner." Jennings mentioned something of his process in 1833 when he declared that he has "gentlemen's garments scoured on his patent plan, which is executed by process of steam, and gives them the polish and appearance of new." H. Levett advertised in 1840 that at his place men's clothing was "cleaned and repaired at shortest notice." Such second-hand dealers as George Levie, J. G. Myers, and Thomas D. Conroy performed similar services.[42]

The Clothing Houses of New York. By the 1840's and 1850's a number of the metropolitan wholesalers had assumed such size and stature that their very existence assured and intensified the central position of the New York clothing market.

From the points of view of personnel and organization, these early firms had much in common. They were generally partnerships of three or four men, who were frequently related through familial ties. In most cases their founders were second- and third-generation Americans, a number of whom were of Yankee (New England) stock and all of whom displayed a strong talent for organizing huge enterprises efficiently. And their plants and showrooms were housed in imposing structures of four to seven stories situated in the heart of the downtown business district.

Let us look for a moment at 87 Chambers Street, where was located one of the leading New York firms, C. T. Longstreet and Co. Before 1846, Longstreet, the senior partner in the firm, was engaged as a merchant tailor in Syracuse. In 1846 he moved to New York where, together with two partners, he began wholesale operations. By 1850 he had accumulated a sufficient amount of money to retire. In 1852 he did retire, leaving the business in the hands of his partners and returning to Syracuse. But "to minds like his, a life of ease and idleness is impossible; hence, in 1855 we found him again in his late theatre of successful action, busily engaged in organizing a new model establishment."[43] By 1856 the firm was ideally organized. Since it was composed of a number of partners, all of whom had many years of experience, each was placed at the head of one section of the enterprise, while Longstreet acted as supreme overseer. "Thus one member of the firm makes the purchases, another attends to manufacturing, a third superintends the sales department, a fourth has charge of the books and correspondence, while Mr. Longstreet has a general supervision over the transactions of the house." At 87 Chambers Street the firm constructed an imposing building seven floors high and "150 feet deep, running through to No. 69 Reade Street." The firm's efficient organization, together with its liberal credit policy, made it most attractive to the visiting merchants.

Equally attractive was the large house of Daniel Devlin and Co., which, although it had gone through a series of reorganizations—it was D. J. Devlin and Co. in 1848, D. Devlin and Co. in 1855, and Devlin Hudson and Co. in 1860—remained one of the leaders in the industry throughout the 1840's and 1850's. The firm was especially noted for its successful efforts in establishing a name for itself not only as a wholesale house but also as a retail, custom, and men's furnishings dealer. Its idea of handling all four branches of men's wear was subsequently imitated by many other houses. Each floor of the Devlin firm—which in 1848 possessed two houses on John Street and a few years later had an imposing structure at 258, 259, and 260 Broadway—was devoted to one field of clothing. In the John Street building "one entire floor" was "devoted to the city and retail business; another to the cloth and custom department; another to the wholesale department; another containing several well-lighted rooms, to the cutting department; and the large basement" was "stored with their immense stock of heavy woolens and trimmings." Each department in turn was divided into a number of parts: "their cutters" were "classified into four departments; one department exclusively for coats; a second for pants; a third for vests; and a fourth for trimmings." In addition, each department was managed by an expert. The retail department was managed by "the junior partner Mr. Barnum, who, for over twenty years, was chief manager in the large retail concern of Messrs. Brooks & Brothers."[44] In 1858 the firm's building was described as "one of the most beautiful of the many beautiful structures in New York. It is five stories in height, constructed entirely of white marble, and has a frontage of fifty feet on Broadway, and is one hundred and ten feet deep."

The clothing house of Brooks Brothers also served to increase the popularity of the New York industry. Still in existence today, the firm is a classic example of a company that grew slowly but steadily; no mushroom rise can be detected in its history. From a small tailor shop in 1818, it grew to one of the leading houses by 1861. In size, appearance, and number of employees, it strongly resembled the two firms discussed above. It dealt in both clothing and men's furnishings and its control throughout the period remained in the hands of the family. After the death of the elder Brooks in 1833, the firm was placed in the hands of his two sons and was designated H. and D. H. Brooks and Co. In the early 1850's the name was changed to Brooks Brothers, the name it bears today. By 1858 the firm had two imposing stores, one on the site of its former and first location at the corner of Cherry and Catherine streets and the other (which was opened in 1858) at the corner of Broadway and Grand Street.[45]

Also well known to southern and western buyers was the large wholesale house of James Wilde, Jr. In the 1840's and early 1850's Wilde was the senior partner in Wilde, Bates, and Taylor, a clothing firm dissolved in January, 1853. In 1854 Wilde, now in complete charge of a newly-reorganized firm, removed his place of business from its former cramped quarters on Nassau Street to a spacious warehouse with a front on Park Place. Each of the new plant's four floors, as in other large clothing houses of the time, was devoted to a specific aspect of the business. On the first floor was "the counting room and the finer description of goods; the second" was "devoted to medium priced goods, and also to giving out and receiving work; the third to coarser qualities of goods;" and the fourth to the trimming and cutting operations. Wilde, who was originally "a partner in an importing house," arranged for the importation of all of the fabrics himself. The manufacturing was supervised by his partner, Mr. Kirtland. The firm claimed that its "sales extend to every state in the Union and almost every territory." It is not surprising, therefore, that weekly payroll expenses alone amounted to $4,000.[46]

Another attractive New York clothing house was the large firm of Lewis, Chatterton, and Co., whose senior partner, Thomas Chatterton, began his career as a jobber of men's clothing in New Haven in about 1840 and turned to manufacturing in 1846. In 1856 Chatterton decided to make a new home in New York, where he began manufacturing clothing at 60 Liberty Street. Later he moved to larger quarters on Warren Street, where the firm of Lewis, Chatterton, and Co. was eventually housed.[47]

These five firms—Longstreet, Devlin, Brooks, Wilde, and Chatterton—did not extend their retail outlets to the South and West as did a number of other large New York clothiers, such as Hanford and Brother and Alfred Munroe and Co. Nevertheless, the fact that they did remain only in the city, although they were extremely dependent upon the trade with the South and West, is in itself a measure of the pull they exerted on the country buyers. This pull, of course, was strengthened by the fact that the New York houses were among the first to enter the field of manufacturing shirts and men's furnishings for the country buyers.

In 1822 Luke Davies, the founder of the first furnishings house, gave the industry its name of "furnishing goods." His firm, eventually called Luke Davies and Son, was originally located at the corner of William and John streets. A number of the employees trained in that company later left to go into business for themselves. Joseph S. Lowrey, for example, left Davies in 1857 and organized the firm of Lowrey, Donaldson, and Co.

It was in response to the demands of the country buyers that some of the earliest shirt manufacturers were formed in New York. Prior to the 1830's ready-made or "stock shirts" were generally unknown. If shirts were required, they were made according to measurements. One of the first, if not the first, shirt factory in America was established in 1832 by two New York clothing merchants, David and Isaac N. Judson, at the corner of Cherry and Market streets. From 1832 to 1840 the Judsons had the entire shirt manufacturing field to themselves. After 1840 the shirt trade proved so prosperous and stable that other manufacturers were attracted to it. By the mid-1850's the leading manufacturer of men's shirts was the firm of Winchester and Davies, which had its factory in New Haven and an additional office in New York. Its senior partner, John M. Davies, began his career as a shirt manufacturer in the early 1840's when he founded the firm of John M. Davies, Jones, and Co. at 22 Warren Street in New York. Davies' partner-to-be, Oliver F. Winchester, was originally a carpenter in Baltimore. Winchester came to New York City in the mid-1840's, learned the shirt trade, and joined Davies in 1847 to found the New Haven Shirt Manufactory. The success of the firm was undoubtedly due in part to Winchester's inventiveness, which manifested itself in the constant improvement of the ready-made shirt. His inventiveness also manifested itself later in the invention of the rifle that still bears him name. In 1854 the firm of Winchester and Davies produced "an average of 100 dozen shirts daily, of all the different varieties, white and colored and cotton and linen," did "a business of $300,000 per annum," and furnished "employment to about 300 persons in the factory, and 3,700 out of the factory." In addition, the New Haven factory was said to cover about an acre and a half of ground.[48]

By the 1840's and 1850's Boston and Philadelphia were also supporting large clothing establishments. One Boston firm, founded by George

W. Simmons, was compared in 1849 to such New York houses as Devlin and Lewis and Hanford. In Philadelphia, the firm of Messrs. Bennett and Co., founded in 1844 and popularly known as "Bennett's Mamoth Tower Hall Clothing Bazar"—it had a five-story building on Market Street—was a popular resort of the country buyers. Another well-liked Philadelphia firm, also founded in 1844, was F. A. Hoyt and Brother, which was known for its extensive trade in boys' clothing. Hoyt, however, was in many ways dependent upon the New York market, because its senior partner, F. A. Hoyt, was for many years before 1844 connected with a large clothing house in New York City and, after he had established himself in Philadelphia, he continued to purchase cloth and trimmings from his former associates.

Other cities, too, prided themselves on their large clothing houses. For example, Henry Whitman and Co. of Providence bore the proud title, "Hall of Commerce." In addition, the firm of George P. Wilkinson and Co. of Troy, New York, was reputed to be the pioneer house of ready-made clothing in that city. Wilkinson was founded in 1842.[49]

No city, however, offered the New York clothing houses any serious competition in the years before the Civil War, because the city's clothiers were the first in the field and they tended to multiply the most rapidly. Other cities could boast of one or two clothing emporiums, but New York could point to dozens of giants who, by the late 1850's, were together averaging millions of dollars in business per year.

IV

TRADE WITH THE SOUTH

More than any other section of the country the South helped to enrich New York tailors and expand their trade to a point of national leadership. Prior to 1850 a very large proportion of the clothing produced in the city was shipped to the southern cotton producing states and, although after 1850 increasing shipments moved westward, about half of the New York garments continued to head for southern ports. The New York Chamber of Commerce estimated—perhaps overestimated—that about two-thirds of the New York clothing trade in 1858 was done with the southern states.

So important was the early southern market that one early reviewer of the New York industry characterized its very origins as a response to the demand for clothing by southern merchants. Writing of the beginnings of the industry, he declared that "the demand from southern merchants . . . for clothing ready-made . . . soon developed the wholesale clothing business, and prior to 1837 . . . the business was almost wholly confined to the South."[1] New Yorkers, after all, enjoyed doing business with Southerners. "The southern chaps," it was felt, "are A-No.-1. They have generally plenty of money or cotton which is money."[2] This feeling never diminished in the years prior to the Civil War and, more and more, New York became virtually a "southern city" from the point of view of its business transactions.[3]

The New York clothing merchant fitted his dealings very neatly into "the cotton triangle." Packets diverted southern cotton to New York and then sailed to European ports, where the southern produce was exchanged for manufactures that were returned to New York to be distributed to the South and West. As a result, the New York clothier, who was excellently located, easily loaded his produce on the final leg of the triangle. With New York packets making regularly scheduled stops at Charleston, Savannah, Mobile, and New Orleans, the New York clothier was able to establish firm connections and to accept and fill orders for clothing with ease and regularity.

The loading of men's clothing on packets along the East River was an almost daily occurrence. With space limited on and below deck, garments were tightly packed in trunks and bales. The finer apparel was probably packed in trunks, while the cheaper grades were stuffed into bales. Thus, for example, shipments to the Charleston port in the fall of 1825 included a number of trunks containing fine coats, pantaloons, and vests, and a few bales filled with pea and monkey jackets and a variety of flannel and woolen shirts. Similar shipments went to Columbus, Georgia, where some years later a merchant advertised that he had for sale "20 trunks ready-made clothing, from the first establishments in New York."[4]

Shipping rates naturally varied according to demand and space available on board the vessel. Summer rates were about 25 per cent higher than winter rates. In 1835 dry goods shipped to Charleston and Savannah paid between 6 and 8 cents per cubic foot; those shipped to New Orleans and Mobile paid about 12.5 cents per cubic foot.[5]

New Orleans was the chief southern port and a good portion of the clothing was unloaded there. That the garments came from New York by packet steamer was made quite clear in newspaper advertisements. "I shall constantly be receiving," wrote one New Orleans dealer in 1843, "by every packet from New York, large additions to my present stock, and of the most choice and fashionable styles that the New York market can produce." The firm of Norris and Way declared in the early spring of 1847 that it was "constantly receiving by every packet from . . . New York fine fashionable clothing." H. B. Montross and Co. announced that it had "received, by the late arrivals from New York, the following spring goods: superior French merino frock and dress coats . . . croton cloth dress and business coats . . . superior merino pantaloons . . . black satin vests." Folger and Blake claimed in 1846 that in the field of "boys' and children's clothing" they were "now receiving by the packet ships from New York, the largest and best assortment offered." Isaac Hart announced in New Orleans that "Shirts! Shirts! Shirts!" were being unloaded from every packet arriving from New York.[6]

Inadequate Clothing Industry in the South. Since their energy was absorbed in a growing cotton economy, the Southerners made few provisions to clothe their own people. Before 1820 a few signs pointed toward an increasing diversification of economic pursuits in the South and for a while it seemed that small manufactures would be supported and that industrialization would run along lines parallel to those of the North. With the invention of the cotton gin, however, cotton became king and most of the serious attempts at industrialization ceased.

The South's neglected craft of tailoring was dominated mostly by Negroes, either slave or free, and by white Northerners who moved into southern urban centers. The Southerners themselves had little regard for this calling. In 1850 New Orleans had 82 free colored tailors, of whom 3 were Negroes and 79 Mulattoes, and Charleston had 87 free Negro tailors. A few years later Charleston counted 78 male Negro tailors, 36 of whom were slaves; 88 Negro seamstresses, 20 of whom were slaves; and 6 free Negro tailoresses.[7]

The frequent public sales of tailors, tailoresses, and seamstresses certainly did not add prestige to the calling. The *New Orleans Daily Picayune* announced two such sales in 1847, advertising "an accomplished Negro tailor good character," and a "seamstress for sale . . . cutter and maker of ladies' and children's clothes, gentlemen's shirts, & etc. in the best style. She is about 22 years of age and fully guaranteed." As a result, white artisans were "doubly injured by a competition against which it is hopeless to contend, and by the stigma which prejudice affixed to all employments that are occupied by slaves."

Efforts by each of a number of southern states to launch its own clothing industry were, nevertheless, evident by the 1850's. In New Orleans in 1852 A. Rose claimed to have "200 tailors constantly employed." In 1859 Charles Lamm of New Orleans tried to belittle the New York product: his clothing, he felt, was not only "better made" but also was lower in price and more elegant in style "than the most of what is manufactured at the North." By "making it himself," he added, he could "afford to sell it at retail at as moderate rate as the large establishments." In Nashville in 1857 R. H. Brockway and Co. declared in verse that

"Here may be found a splendid stock;
Why go to Boston or New York?
To order here your clothes are made;
Why not support your southern trade?
A hundred hands or more will say
Work here at home and get good pay.
This good example shows the way
We make our bread from day to day."[8]

In Nashville "Nathan's Clothing Manufactory Store" boasted an assortment of ready-made clothing of its own manufacture.[9] In the years prior to the Civil War Virginia had two extensive manufactories. The first, Baldwin and Co., which could trace its origins to 1838 in Richmond, was by 1856 supplying eight houses in Virginia and North Carolina with clothing.[10] The second was the firm of A. S. Shafer and Co. of Petersburg, which also supplied "a very large trade in Virginia and North Carolina."

Yet both of those firms would have found it difficult to survive without the strong connections they continued to maintain with the New York market. Since Baldwin was associated with the house of Keen & Scott in Newark, New Jersey, it had "every advantage of the New York market, which a northern house can have." Shafer was connected with Halsey, Hunter & Co., also in Newark. Halsey attended to purchases in the North, "constantly watching the New York markets, from which he selects and forwards the latest styles as soon as they appear."

Thus, some strides were made in establishing a clothing industry in the South. But the total value of the products of the entire region—Virginia, North Carolina, South Carolina, Georgia, Florida, Alabama, Mississippi, Louisiana, Texas, Arkansas, and Tennessee—came nowhere near the product value of New York State, which alone in 1860 produced clothing valued at more than $25,000,000. That year the southern products were valued at less than $3,000,000. In 1860 the entire South had only 352 establishments, which employed 1,038 men and 681 women, and nearly two-thirds of the region's production, according to the census report of that year, took place in Louisiana, which produced clothing valued at $1,707,072. The greatest rate of increase also took place in Louisiana, which, between 1850 and 1860, increased its production by 402.3 percent. The increase in Mississippi, which was second greatest, amounted to 222.8 per cent. Most of the southern states, however, produced little clothing in 1860: Florida produced an annual value of $5,000, North Carolina produced $12,370, and South Carolina produced $44,960.

Clothing Importations in the South. It is not surprising that southern cities turned to countries abroad for part of their supply. Next to New York and San Francisco, New Orleans was the largest center of clothing importation in the years from 1855 to 1860: it imported a value of $94,272 in 1855-1856 and $115,530 in 1859-1860. Since the total national value ranged only between $300,000 and $400,000 for each of these years, New Orleans' imports were substantial. Much smaller amounts entered the ports of Charleston and Mobile: Charleston imported clothing valued at somewhere between $630 and $1,165 for each of the years between 1855 and 1860 and Mobile imported even less.

Obviously, imports of ready-made garments played a very minor part in clothing the American people. Even if the total imports of the United States had been offered to the South, they would have failed to satisfy that region's need for clothing. As a result, the South looked to the domestic market for its supply.

Clothing Auctions in the South. Once clothing had been moved from

New York City to a southern port, a portion of it was thrown into auction for sale to the country retailers, many of whom could not afford the trip to New York. The auctions were not, however, devoted completely to the New York product; some imported garments and various products of other cities were also sold. The auctioneers announced in advance the origin of the clothing to be sold, stating clearly at times whether the stock was foreign or American.

Southern auctioneers at times visited New York to solicit business from manufacturers. In 1860 William H. Barnes went to New York City from Atlanta to represent his "Model Auction House," an institution he described as having "two immense salesrooms, each subdivided to receive different varieties of goods." In New York he solicited large consignments of clothing.[11]

New Orleans, the chief distributing center in the South, was also the seat of the most numerous clothing auctions in the area. Auction rooms, however, did not exist in New Orleans prior to the 1840's. Instead, unconsigned cargoes were disposed of on a personal basis between ship captains and buyers along the wharves.[12] Later numerous public auction stores were set up and a number of them devoted many hours to the sale of clothing. Popular among the New Orleans clothing auctioneers were the firms of Sykes & Hyde (later reorganized first under the name of H. Peychaud, Hyde & Co. and then under E. Roger & Co.), Francis Fernandez & Whiting, Blache & Leamont, J. L. Taylor & Co., and Vincent & Co.

As in a New York auction the time and place of the sale, a description of the goods to be auctioned, and an invitation to examine the clothing before the sale were published in the local newspapers. A large variety of qualities and styles of clothing was presented at these auctions. There were cases of "blanket coats, monkey jackets . . . cashmere vests, hickory and flannel shirts" and clothing for children, field hands, and fashionable gentlemen. Garments were disposed of in cases, trunks, lots, dozens, or pairs. At times goods were "sold in lots to suit purchasers." Every accommodation was offered to the country purchasers who flocked to New Orleans to purchase northern products.

The Southern Storekeeper. It was from the shelves of the storekeeper's shop that most southern consumers obtained their New York garments. Stocking ready-made clothing in the general store became a popular practice in the South as early as the beginning of the nineteenth century. In their advertisements storekeepers constantly listed the variety of goods available at their shops. That the stock had been purchased originally in New York was in most cases clearly stated.[13]

After 1820 there was a tendency for the ready-made clothing departments to break away from the general store and every southern center of population soon had numerous clothing stores. Charleston counted 9 clothing stores in 1828. New Orleans listed 56 hat, shoe, and clothing stores in its city directory in 1822 and 110 clothing stores, 13 merchant tailor shops, and 66 tailors in 1838. Atlanta, which probably had no more than 5,000 inhabitants in 1851, listed a clothing store operated by William Herring and Son and two independent merchant tailors. Small towns in Tennessee each had a few dealers in clothing in 1857: Memphis had 29, Shelbyville had 2, Knoxville had 4, and Chattanooga had 2, and Clarksville had 2 merchant tailors. Nashville alone in 1860 listed 42 clothing stores, 8 wholesale dealers in clothing, 14 merchant tailors, and 20 tailors.[14]

Although many dealers were listed as "merchant tailors" or "tailors," their time was not devoted solely to the craft of tailoring. Many spent much of their time distributing clothing that they had picked up either directly or indirectly from the New York market. L. Fitch & Co. of Macon, Georgia, listed itself as "merchant tailors," but its advertisements show that its representatives made frequent trips to the North to purchase ready-made clothing. This practice was followed by tailors in other southern cities, too. In fact, it has been suggested that dealing in ready-made clothing proved so lucrative that many southern tailors dropped their needles and turned exclusively to buying and selling.

In smaller southern towns the general storekeeper found it profitable to stock ready-made garments among his other wares. George W. Dillingham, a country merchant in Columbus, Georgia, in 1834 sold leather, shot, sugar, and "20 trunks ready-made clothing, from the first establishments in New York." The stock of a country store auctioned in New Orleans in 1857 consisted "in part of . . . camlet Jeans, summer Paletot coats and pants, white and colored shirts . . . and a variety of other articles."

That the clothing sold was a product of New York was a point always stressed by dealers of men's apparel in the South. The proprietors of the Fashionable Clothing & Hat Store in Columbus, Georgia, declared in 1834 that they had "just returned from New York, with a splendid assortment" of ready-made clothing, consisting in part of "coats and frocks, of superior workmanship" as well as "black, blue and fancy stripe cashmere pantaloons." A. Dulin advertised in Atlanta in 1847 that he had "just opened a fine assortment of goods recently purchased in New York, consisting in part of . . . a choice lot of ready-made clothing." In 1845 J. W. Knapps opened for sale in Baton Rouge "direct from the manufactory in New York" clothing for boys "suitable for youths and children, from five to fifteen." One proprietor in New Orleans actually named his establishment the "New York Clothing Store."

New York Manufacturers in the South. The strength of the New York clothing industry lay partly in the fact that its founders did not rely exclusively upon orders placed by visiting southern merchants; rather, they moved into southern cities to establish their own outlets. As early as the 1820's a number of New York manufacturers had opened retail outlets in the South. In 1828 one manufacturer, a Mr. Rowe, was said to have "a great establishment at New Orleans" and "six or eight men to cut out clothes, and 200 or 300 tailoresses to make them up" in New York.[15]

A few dealers moved into the South indirectly—that is, they entered the clothing business in a southern city and then moved to New York to manufacture garments for a market with which they were already well acquainted. George Opdyke, who during the Civil War became mayor of New York, lived in New Orleans for five years before he came to New York in 1832 to become a wholesale manufacturer of men's clothing on Hudson Street. Together with his brother-in-law, John D. Scott, Opdyke formed a partnership called John D. Scott & Co. The firm eventually opened three retail stores in New Orleans, Charleston, and Memphis.[16]

Joseph Seligman, who arrived in the U.S. in 1838, became a cashier in a Philadelphia bank, saved his money, and moved to Greensburg, Alabama, where he opened a clothing store. A few years later he moved to New York, where he became a wholesale dealer on Church Street. The firm of Hora and Mann at 250 Pearl Street claimed in an advertisement that its ability to produce clothing suitable for the southern market lay in the fact that it had "carried on the clothing business for a number of years at the South."

New Orleans was the chief target of the majority of the New York clothiers. Establishing an outlet in New Orleans meant gaining a foothold in the chief commercial center of the South. Newspapers of that city were covered with announcements of New York clothiers who had retail outlets there. One of the most vocal dealers was Alfred Munroe, who, like other New York wholesalers, opened a place of business near the waterfront on New Orleans' Magazine Street. Munroe, too, had felt out the southern market before moving into New York as a manufacturer of men's garments in 1847. In that year he began announcing in New Orleans that all merchandise sold at his "one price retail clothing establishment" was manufactured in his New York factory "expressly for . . . retail sales here."[17] Prior to 1847 Munroe had constantly received huge shipments of New York clothing not of his own manufacture. After that date the firm, now called Alfred Munroe and Co., maintained a plant at 441 Broadway in New York City and a large retail store at 34 Magazine Street in New Orleans. One of Munroe's two partners, William D. Abbot, managed the New York branch, and the other, James Mushaway, maintained permanent residence in New Orleans and took charge of the southern outlet. In the Magazine Street store Munroe maintained a huge stock of clothing. In 1847 his advertisements claimed a stock valued at $50,000. In 1848 he advertised "$60,000 worth of clothing at retail" and challenged "the world to show, in one store, an assortment equal" to his, which included 2,300 coats, 1,900 pantaloons, 1,500 vests, and 8,000 shirts. Three years later he announced that shipments from New York had brought "an immense addition to our previous stock," that there was $90,000 worth of clothing selling at retail in his New Orleans store, and that, as a result of the immense variety of merchandise, he could "fit persons of all sizes, from a man measuring forty-eight (48) inches to a child." By 1854 Munroe had attained a national reputation as a manufacturer of boys' clothing and had received a prize medal at the Crystal Palace exhibition, America's first World's Fair, in New York City.[18] Munroe made every effort to enlarge its share of the New Orleans trade. "For the accommodation of those of our customers who are unable to call during the day," announced one of its advertisements, "we keep our store open in the evening, until half-past 9 o'clock."

The outbreak of the Mexican War proved very profitable to the warehouses of New Orleans, which were called upon to supply an intensified demand for all kinds of merchandise. Munroe offered clothing to all those going to and returning from the Mexican theater of action. The firm also took advantage of the added business stimulated by the rush to the California gold fields in 1849. "Take a good supply of clothing with you," announced one of its advertisements "to the California gold diggers." The firm promoted clothing especially suited for the forty-niners, such as "India rubber clothing," hunting jackets, and coats, as well as "red and white flannel shirts and drawers."

It was upon the needs of the well dressed southern gentlemen, however, that Munroe mainly relied. "Who goes to the ball or party tonight?" asked Munroe, who in 1847 said that at his store gentlemen could be supplied with "rich gold and silver figured silk velvet vests," as well as with other fashionable New York garments. Since Munroe and his agent shuttled between the New York factory and the New Orleans store, it was a simple matter to keep New Orleans up to date with New York City modes. In fact, a special service that Munroe offered to his southern patrons—a service extended by other New York-New Orleans clothiers, too—was that of making a garment in New York according to measurements taken in New Orleans. The firm also included in its retail stock garments not of its own manufacture. For example, it took advantage of the growing popularity of waterproof rubber clothing in the 1850's; the Magazine Street store became the distributing agent of "vulcanized India rubber goods" manufactured by the Union India Rubber Co. of New York.[45]

The steady expansion of its New York and New Orleans facilities is the proof of Munroe's success. During the summer of 1848 the New Orleans store was enlarged. In 1860 it was moved out of 34 Magazine Street to the "Story Building" at the corner of Camp and Common streets, which it called the Palace Clothing Store. In New York the firm opened a new retail outlet under the popular St. Nicholas Hotel at 307 Broadway. In addition, by that time, another partner, M. G. Rathbum, had entered the firm.[19] Although the 1857 crisis forced the partnership to knock down prices—a practice long avoided–it did not seem to put a permanent dent in the firm, which continued its southern activity with full vigor until the outbreak of war.

A few doors away from the Munroe store—at 43 Magazine Street in New Orleans—was the "New Clothing and Shirt Warehouse" of Lewis and Hanford, large New York wholesalers. Unlike Munroe, the Hanford firm had established in New Orleans a primarily wholesale outlet for its New York product. Although its advertisements were far more modestly worded and appeared far less frequently than those of Munroe, the extent of its operations was probably far greater. By the mid-1850's the Hanford firm, by then renamed Hanford and Brother, was "reputed to be the most extensive manufacturer of clothing in the United States."

Hanford could trace its origins to Boston, where operations were begun in 1825 by Mr. Lewis. In 1834 Lewis moved to New York City, where he was joined in 1840 by S. H. Hanford, with whom he formed the partnership of Lewis and Hanford. Located on busy Pearl Street, where it soon acquired the impressive address of 252, 254, 256, and 258, the firm by 1848 had attained the reputation of being one of the leading distributors to the South and claimed a labor force of nearly 5,000. Its four New York stores consisted of "thirteen spacious rooms," five used as salesrooms, "three for coats, pants and vests, two for . . . shirts and drawers, and one as a packing department . . . [and] two . . . rooms for cutting and trimming." A visitor to the firm in 1856 was "struck with the perfect order and system so manifest in every department of the business." After the death of Lewis in 1850 Hanford was joined by his brother, John, and the firm was renamed Hanford and Brother. In 1858 John H. Browning formed with John E. Hanford a partnership called Hanford and Browning, the predecessor of the modern Browning, King and Co.[20]

Next door to Alfred Munroe and three doors away from the Hanford outlet—at 36 Magazine Street in New Orleans—in the early 1840's was another clothing merchant, H. B. Montross. Montross constantly received New York clothing, which he retailed and wholesaled to surrounding southern consumers and merchants. At the same time, at 112 Fulton Street in New York City, Sylvanus B. Stilwell was manufacturing clothing largely for the southern market. Stilwell, a native of Long Island, "began life as a tailor, with an empty pocket," but, through "sterling honesty, industry and economy . . . overcame all difficulties, and, in 1840, established a clothing house" in New York. A few years later Stilwell and Montross met, perhaps during one of Montross' annual visits to New York, and formed a partnership called Montross and Stilwell. Montross moved his New Orleans store to 19 Magazine Street and from 1847 on the partners' business cards always displayed both addresses—"Montross & Stilwell, wholesale and retail Dealers in Clothing, No. 19 Magazine Street, New Orleans, No. 112 Fulton Street, New York."[21]

The firm wholesaled and retailed men's clothing and furnishings of various qualities and styles, advertising a "large and superior assortment of fine and fashionable clothing" and a "large stock for country trade." It also reminded merchants about to depart for New York of the establishment's main office in that city and invited them "to call and examine our stock, which cannot be excelled in style and material." In addition, the firm pointed out that orders did not have to be placed in New York and that "friends from the country may depend upon their orders being filled" if placed at the Magazine Street outlet.

To southern gentlemen the firm offered this service, similar to that offered by Munroe, in 1850: "gentlemen in want of clothes for their own wear are invited to leave their orders and measure" at the Magazine Street store, from where they were sent to Fulton Street for manufacture and to where they were quickly returned. Like other New York manufacturers dealing with the South, Montross and Stilwell tried to do a cash business in their retail operations. They even called their southern outlet the Cash Clothing Establishment. Cash transactions were impossible, however, when the country merchants placed wholesale orders. The firm's terms, in fact, were "for goods at retail, cash; at wholesale, cash or city paper." Did the partnership prove prosperous? A survey of wealth in New York City in 1855 showed that Sylvanus B. Stilwell was worth $175,000, no small sum in the years preceding the Civil War.

Numerous other New York firms also branched out to New Orleans; in many ways each had a similar organization and background. The clothing house of Taylor and Hadden, which had a factory first at 69 John Street and later at 249 Pearl Street in New York City, retailed and wholesaled in the South throughout the 1840's and 1850's. In New Orleans its store was first located on Chartres Street; in 1843, however, it was moved to Magazine Street, which became almost an extension of the New York clothing district. Prior to 1848 the business consisted of the two partners: C. Hadden, who maintained permanent residence in New York, where he supervised manufacturing and wholesale operations; and Z. Taylor, who remained as overseer of the New Orleans store. In 1848 a third partner, C. C. Carter, was brought into the firm to remain in New Orleans in order to work with Taylor. In 1852 the firm, then called Taylor, Hadden and Co., moved from Magazine Street around the corner to 66 Canal Street.[23]

A few doors away, at 44 Canal Street, was another New York-New Orleans clothier, Thompson and Nixon. Thompson, the senior partner, supervised the factory at 87 Cedar Street in New York. Nixon remained in New Orleans to look after the sales of "dress coats . . . frock coats . . . fancy coats . . . sack coats . . . pantaloons . . . vests." He also frequently visited New York, always announcing his departure in advance so that all who wanted to place orders could be sure that he would "attend personally to their execution." Thus, he carried to New York the measurements of his New Orleans customers and returned with the finished garments. Unlike other houses, Thompson and Nixon concentrated largely upon retail trade in New Orleans. In New York in 1851 it opened a new retail store on Broadway called Thompson, Peck & Nixon's Tailoring and Furnishing Store. Peck, a third partner, had joined the business. In 1851 the firm also moved its New Orleans outlet from Canal Street to 19 Camp Street.

Two doors away, at 22 Camp Street, was the New York outlet of Norris and Way, which also specialized in retailing men's clothing. A member of this firm also announced his frequent departures to the

North. On June 16, 1847, the *New Orleans Daily Picayune* carried the following advertisement:

"NOTICE—Our customers and others, who would like to have their clothing for next fall got out expressly to their order, will please call at our store before the 1st of July next and have their measure taken and leave their orders.

"One of the members of the firm will go North at that time, and will give his personal attention to the orders with which we shall be favored.

"They are taken with the express understanding that if the goods do not give perfect satisfaction to the persons who order them they are under no obligation to take them."[24]

All measurements taken were carefully filed and, before the beginning of each season, orders were solicited for new styles. Thus, in the summer of 1848, the firm asked that "the gentlemen whose measures we have . . . please call and give their orders for the clothing they desire for next fall and winter." Because no New York address was given by Norris and Way, one suspects that it might have acted as distributors for a number of New York firms that could not themselves afford to establish retail outlets in New Orleans. The firm disbanded in 1857. Later reorganized as Norris Maull and Co., it maintained a manufactory in Philadelphia.[25]

How numerous the New York clothiers became in New Orleans in the 1850's can be seen in one of that city's directories. Included were such houses as Francis Fabre and Co., which had a store below the St. Charles Hotel in New Orleans and a factory in New York; J. L. Bach and Co., which manufactured clothing in New York under the direction of Bach and conducted a wholesale and retail outlet in New Orleans under the supervision of S. Jacob and Judah Hart; Gensler and Simon; Scott and Searing; and T. Surges and Co.[26]

The directory failed to mention some shirt manufacturers, who, according to their advertisements, seem to have been equally prominent in New Orleans. Since the production of shirts was emerging as a business separate from the manufacture of ready-made clothing, listings of clothing dealers frequently failed to mention the shirt manufacturers.

One, Charles Leighton, was in 1846 producing shirts in New York and distributing them in New Orleans. Some years later Leighton opened a second store in New Orleans. Doing business with the South proved so profitable for him that by 1854 he had expanded into the clothing business and had taken over the partnership of Thompson and Nixon, changing the firm's name to Leighton and Barbot. The name was changed to Leighton and Blanc in 1860.

Like Alfred Munroe and other dealers, Leighton tried to adhere to a one-price policy when selling at retail. He called his store in 1848 "The Six-Day, One-Price Shirt Store" because it was open every day but Sunday. Since other New Orleans stores were open on Sunday, Leighton stayed open as late as possible on Saturday—until eleven o'clock at night—hoping to scoop up a great deal of the Sunday trade.

At 15 Camp Street was the New Orleans Shirt Depot, the southern outlet of a New York shirt manufactory located at 73 William Street. Its owner and manager, Isaac Hart, was for many years active in business, social, and philanthropic affairs in New Orleans. Always reminding his customers of his immense stock—which in October, 1847, included 5,000 linen, 20,000 muslin, 3,000 colored, and 5,000 check and plantation shirts—he also always mentioned that his stock was constantly being enlarged by recent arrivals from his New York manufactory.[27]

Canal Street in New Orleans housed two other New York shirt manufacturers. The first was a Mr. Charpentier, who arrived from France in the mid-1840's and opened a factory at 82 Broadway in New York and a retail and wholesale depot in New Orleans. Charpentier claimed to be an "inventor of an entirely new system of cutting shirts, collars, undershirts and drawers," a technique which he perfected while a shirtmaker in Paris.[28]

The second was S. N. Moody, a wholesaler and retailer of shirts manufactured at his plant at 381 Broadway in New York. Constantly priding himself on his huge stock, Moody was prepared to sell shirts of "any quality, any pattern, any size, any price." He claimed that he took frequent trips to New York, where he personally supervised all manufacturing processes. Moody survived the financial crisis of 1857 and by 1860 he had devised a system of "self-measurement," which he "sent by post" to all who desired to order his shirts by mail.

Clothing the Southern Slave. Providing clothing for the plantation Negro was not the prime function of the New York clothier and the advertisements in southern newspapers stressed the sale of fashionable clothing from New York, not clothing for slaves. Numerous sources other than the New York market, however, were open to the planter for clothing his bondsmen.

Many of the southern plantations were organized so that much of the clothing worn by the slaves was produced right on the premises, often by the slaves themselves. The planters were generally stingy about providing sufficient clothing for their bondsmen, because plantation economy dictated that only a minimum expenditure be made in this area. It was only on special occasions, such as holidays, that the slaves were dressed in brighter and more expensive costumes.[29] Reports on plantation management, however, did occasionally stress the importance of clothing the Negro properly at least for the sake of health and efficiency. It was generally agreed by experienced plantation managers that three or four suits should be allotted to each slave each year.[30] Nevertheless, heavy outlays of cash for ready-made clothing for slaves was a practice that the planters entered into with only the greatest reluctance. Advertisements of "Negro clothing" seldom referred to ready-made clothing; rather, they meant cheap, coarse fabrics from which clothing for Negroes could be made. In their local journals the planters sometimes exchanged ideas about improving the durability of the Negroes' clothing. In 1852 the *Natchez Free Trader* discussed a process of making waterproof socks for "a plantation of 50 or 100 Negroes."

The few manufacturers of ready-made clothing that did begin to emerge in the South and West found it far easier to compete with the New York producer in the field of Negro clothing than to launch into the production of fashionable garments. A New York label on a ready-made suit for a Negro field hand was not a very important item. In a discussion of the growth of the clothing industry in Cincinnati between 1830 and 1860, the commissioner of statistics of the State of Ohio said that one of the important causes for the advance was "the growing demand for cheap clothing to supply farm hands and Negro slaves." The proprietor of the Louisiana Plantation Clothing Manufactory, located in New Orleans, announced to "southern planters" in 1856 that he had "completed his arrangements for the manufacture of plantation clothing on a very large scale" and therefore took "pleasure in informing his country friends and southern planters, that he is . . . prepared to supply them . . . with ready-made Negro clothing . . . at as low prices as articles . . . of northern manufacturers." That Negro clothing was being produced by southerners themselves was also recognized by I. M. Singer and Co., which turned to southern newspapers to announce its "new improved Sewing Machine especially adapted to the making up of Negro clothing."

In addition, the export figures of the ready-made clothing from British ports between 1833 and 1838 show that a good portion of the shipments went under the heading of "slops and Negro clothing."[31]

The South did, however, depend on New York manufacturers for at least part of its supply of ready-made garments for slaves. The Macon Clothing Store advertised in 1826 "a large assortment of Negro clothing" recently received from the North. A few years later the New York

City clothing house of Young and Van Eps called the attention of visiting southern merchants to its stock of ready-made Negro clothing.[32]

In New Orleans Alfred Munroe occasionally advertised such clothing for Negroes as "hickory, check and Negro shirts." The most convincing advertisements, however, were those of Folger and Blake, who appeared to be specialists in this trade and who had abundant stocks of monkey jackets, round jackets, flannel and hickory shirts, and "cottonade suits for small Negroes." This firm constantly reminded planters that they would "find it greatly to their advantage to purchase their clothing ready-made." Located on Magazine Street, Folger and Blake was probably well known to the planters throughout the 1840's and 1850's.

The Crisis of 1860-1861. Further evidence of the importance of the Southern trade to the manufacturers can be seen in the temporary collapse of the New York market that occurred as soon as southern orders dwindled during the political crisis that preceded the Civil War. The southern consumer had assumed a special significance during the panic of 1857 and the two-year depression that followed. With the West largely prostrated, the New York manufacturers and wholesalers had poured their accumulated stocks upon the South, a region which even in those trying years continued to pay its debts.

On New Year's Day in 1859 the *New York Daily Times* declared that the crisis of 1857 had "become almost a matter of history." Moreover, in the spring that followed, business activity and employment in New York City reached a new peak. In addition, a need for crops in Europe helped to turn the western debtors into confident farmers who once again drew upon New York City for needed merchandise. Nevertheless, all was not rosy.

As the movement for abolition gained momentum in the North a number of southern merchants became increasingly cautious in their dealings with New York firms. John Brown's raid at Harpers Ferry in October, 1859, kindled a wave of resentment throughout the South and there was a greater reluctance about traveling North for the spring's purchases. Some firms even cancelled orders already placed. Northern establishments suspected of any abolitionist leanings were blacklisted and in the spring of 1860 an *Advertising Directory for Southern Merchants* was issued. "A guide for southern merchants who must obtain supplies from northern cities," it contained 120 pages and included only businesses reputed to be "friends of the South."[33] The New York wholesalers were generally sympathetic with the South's feelings. Since these Northerners were bound economically with the South, abolitionism proved as abhorrent to them as it did to the slaveholders. As a result, New York merchants shied away from any movement that might give offense to their southern customers and went as far as to advise their workers in November, 1860, not to vote the Republican ticket.[34] But New York City was powerless to affect the vote of even its own state, which gave a majority to Abraham Lincoln.

No sooner was Lincoln elected than a severe depression settled upon the New York clothing industry. The crisis, however, was not due entirely to politics: throughout the summer and fall of 1860 adverse weather conditions in the South destroyed fortunes in wheat, corn, and cotton, and the impoverished southern merchants were forced to cut down on their orders of northern garments. Moody, the New Orleans shirt dealer, announced drastic reductions of prices in October, 1860, attributing the action to "short crops and dull times." Agricultural sluggishness, coupled with the fear of a Republican victory, turned excellent southern customers into reluctant buyers. Moreover, northern merchants were reluctant to extend credit to southern storekeepers at a time when rumors were circulated that should Lincoln be elected, no Southerner would pay his debts. In fact, uncertainty and fear of repudiation did more than anything else to bring on the depression.

With the Republican victory a fact and preparation of the South for secession under way, a severe crisis settled upon the New York clothing industry. There was an immediate drastic reduction in the importation of dry goods into New York. Imports dwindled from a value of $1,993,963 in 1859 to $972,824 in 1860 and to $466,075 in 1861.[35] The *New York Herald* blamed the crisis directly upon the election of Lincoln. After dispatching "a reporter to visit the different factories and firms," it reported that "the result of his investigation" showed "that since the 6th of November there has been an alarming falling off in the sale and manufacture of articles dependent to any great extent upon Southern trade . . . not less than fifteen thousand operatives have already been discharged, and are out of employment at this critical time." It added that "not only have orders ceased to come from the South, but many orders on the books of our manufacturers, varying in amount from $5,000 to $25,000 have been recently countermanded."[36] The newspaper also made this thorough investigation of the New York industry:

"The falling off in the clothing trade with the South amounts to a complete panic. The largest manufacturing houses in the City, which are usually overrun with work at this time of the year for the Southern market, are now doing so little that they have been obliged to discharge at least three-fourths of their workmen. The number so discharged is fully three thousand.

"Messrs. Payan, Carhart & Co., No. 55 Hudson Street, still continue to receive and fill Southern orders; but they are not making up goods as they usually do at this time of year. They have been obliged, in consequence of the aspect of affairs at the South, to discharge nearly one-third of their force . . .

"Messrs. McGrath, Tweed & Co., No. 101 Chambers Street, have been compelled to make a large reduction in their force, and are doing almost nothing in the way of manufacturing. They are usually busy at this time.

"Messrs. O. B. Tweedy & Co., No. 128 Duane Street, have half their usual force of cutters employed, and will make up about half of their usual stock for next season. They did not consider it prudent, in view of existing affairs, to make up more.

"Messrs. Devlin, Hudson & Co., corner of Broadway and Warren Street, have a large Southern trade in clothing, which was very active till the first week in November. From that time their orders from the South began to fall off, and have now entirely ceased. They are now doing literally nothing in the way of sending goods to the South, and depend altogether on their local trade, which is also very large.

"A house in Warren Street, which deals very largely in tailor's trimmings, do not sell ten per cent of their usual sales at this time of the year. They supply large manufacturing houses which make clothing for the South; and . . . their establishments are now idle . .

"Messrs. John Paret & Son, 350 Broadway, and J. D. Scott & Co., 37 Chambers Street, are making up a stock lighter than usual, in consequence of the existing state of affairs at the South.

"Messrs. J. Wilde & Co., 388 Broadway, employ half their usual number of hands, and will make up half their usual stock . . . Fourteen other houses have made large reductions in their force, the encouragement for the trade for the next season being so slim."[37]

Of all the clothing houses surveyed only two were found to be maintaining their optimism and continuing production at the old rate. The first, Lewis B. Brown and Co., which had "a branch house at the South," was reported to "have about their usual force employed" and to intend to "make up their usual stock, if matters at the South become no worse." The second, Longstreet, Bradford, and Co. at 348 Broadway, was said to have orders from the South and still to be at work. It was also reported that a number of houses had taken extensive orders from southern dealers just prior to the election, but that those orders, "one of $8,000 for clothing," had been rejected as soon as the election results had become known.

As tension mounted, the retailers in the South hastened to sell their stocks as quickly as possible. Alfred Munroe and the others announced sales of men's clothing and furnishings at cost.[38] Once the secession and the Civil War became facts, the New York clothiers lost fortunes not only because of the absence of former customers but also because of southern confiscations, which in the case of Hanford and Browning amounted to more than $500,000. It was not until orders for uniforms came pouring in that the industry was once again able to stand on its feet.

V

TRADE WITH THE WEST

New York producers, who were concerned with the South in the years prior to the Civil War also looked for opportunities to the West, where lay a tremendous underdeveloped area that daily attracted more and more people. Moreover, a need for the manufactures of eastern urban centers was felt in the West just as keenly as it was in the South.

Prior to 1825 and the completion of the Erie Canal, it was questionable whether or not New York would gain domination over the western hinterland as it had over the cotton-growing states. Once the canal was completed, however, it became clear that the route from Albany to the Great Lakes would become a chosen one in the distribution of merchandise to the West. It was not long before steamers shuttled daily between Buffalo and midwestern cities, just as they did between New York and the cotton ports, and soon numerous western retailers and wholesalers made New York the principal depot for their purchases.

With the extension of railroad lines westward from New York, the role of the Erie Canal in transporting clothing was diminished. By the 1850's goods classed as "merchandise"—a title under which clothing went—were shipped westward by railroad. Freezing waters during the winter months hampered canal shipments, but rail connections enabled deliveries to be made rapidly in any season.[1] Moreover, there were two other channels through which New York manufactures could move westward. One was through Philadelphia and Baltimore, whose jobbers purchased goods in the New York market and shipped them westward through those cities' facilities. The other was down and around the East Coast to New Orleans, from where the products were shipped up the Mississippi and Ohio Rivers toward the western wholesale centers. Before the advent of the railroad, low rates and rapid service increased the popularity of the Erie Canal over that of all other routes, because before the construction of the canal it was extremely expensive to ship clothing westward. A ton of merchandise moving from Albany to Buffalo cost between $85 and $100. Clothing, which was transported on wagons in "casks," cost about "$6 a cask." With the construction of the canal these rates toppled downwards.

Apparel moving from New York to Buffalo averaged $7.78 a ton between 1830 and 1850.[2]

Wholesale Centers in the Midwest. Just as the cotton ports served as depots for the distribution of New York clothing to southern inland towns, so did St. Louis and, later, Chicago relay New York manufactures to midwestern country stores.

St. Louis, situated on the banks of the Mississippi a few miles below the mouth of the Missouri and less than 200 miles above the mouth of the Ohio, was in an excellent position to distribute manufactures from the East. As early as 1826 its dealers announced the receipt of ready-made clothing "made in the best manner and in the neatest style" from eastern firms.[3] Commission merchants, such as Fish and Spalding, established offices in St. Louis and devoted their time to transferring the New York clothing and dry goods to the country stores.[4] By the mid-1830's a few St. Louis merchants specialized in clothing. One declared in 1835 that he had made arrangements with clothiers in New York and other eastern cities to receive monthly shipments of the latest eastern styles. Like the dealers in the cotton ports who announced their receipt of clothing via New York packets, the St. Louis merchants advertised the arrival of New York clothing by steamer. In 1849 J. and W. Van Deventer, St. Louis clothing jobbers, said that they had just received "fine winter clothing from New York, per steamers *Avalanche* and *Oswego* . . . which added to our former stock, makes our present stock of good fashionable clothing for the retail trade, unsurpassed, for both quality and quantity. Also, received per same boats, a large addition to our wholesale stock for the country trade, all of which are offered low for cash or approved paper.[5]

Despite its importance as a wholesale center, St. Louis made only a meager attempt to manufacture its own apparel. All of its urban energy seemed to be channeled into "the interchange of the various commodities which enter into the traffic of this vast region—chiefly in the importation of merchandise from New Orleans, and eastern cities, and the shipment of western produce to the southern and Atlantic markets."[6]

Chicago was also important as a wholesale center. When incorporated in 1833 it was still a village of less than 200 inhabitants. Its growth, however, was so rapid that by the 1850's it was already threatening St. Louis for the position of distributing agent of New York merchandise. Its streets were jammed with wholesale houses whose success depended largely upon the growing popularity of the railway transportation that soon became centered there. Before 1852 Chicago was an unimportant center for the distribution of clothing. A few general dealers did exist, but the products they handled were low grade. The better grades went to St. Louis. That year, however, Henry A. Huntington put Chicago on the map as an important jobbing center for clothing by establishing the first wholesale house in that city. He stocked his warehouse with an enormous amount of goods and associated himself with two other men to form the firm of Huntington, Wadsworth, and Parks. By 1853 his sales amounted to $140,000. As a result, it was not long before country buyers began to flock to Chicago. By 1859 selling ready-made clothing, most of which was brought from the East, emerged as one of the most important businesses in Chicago, which had six large wholesale houses whose combined sales totaled $2,000,000.[7]

Thus, it was first by ship to St. Louis and later by railway to Chicago that New York clothing arrived in the Midwest. As in the South, clothing sold in the Midwest was seldom paid for with cash. Much of the business transacted between the country merchants and the eastern wholesalers, as well as between the country merchants and their rural customers, was on a credit basis. Clothing dealers in St. Louis, such as the Van Deventers, offered their New York merchandise for "cash or approved paper" and generally had to settle for the latter or worse, such as crops or land. In 1860 a western wholesaler advertised in a New York paper a stock of clothing "adapted [for] the West, for which $2,000 in cash and balance in valuable selected pine timbered and farming lands in Wisconsin will be paid."

New York Manufacturers in the Midwest. The New York manufacturers, who did not rely solely upon the visiting jobbers and storekeepers from the South and who erected outlets in southern cities, followed a similar pattern in the West. Since St. Louis was the chief commercial center for New York in the West, it was there that a number of New York clothiers opened branches. Although the New York tailors sensed the economic value of St. Louis as early as 1820, when a few actually moved there, the large wholesalers did not establish outlets there until after 1840. Pioneer wholesalers included C. and T. Lewis, John T. Martin, and William Seligman. Seligman was a member of a family of dry goods and clothing merchants who had outlets in the South and a large dry goods business in New York City. His brothers, Joseph and James, operated the New York firm, which was on William Street,[8] and sent supplies to St. Louis.

One of the largest outlets in St. Louis belonged to the New York firm of Ticknor, Robbins, and Co., which had in its branch store at

176 North Main Street a large stock of "fine ready-made clothing, and gentlemen's furnishing goods." In one St. Louis advertisement it declared that its "manufactory is located in New York City, and the branch here is but an emporium for the sale of ready-made goods." One member of the firm was stationed in New York to supervise the manufacturing. The depression of the late 1850's did not seem to hamper the firm's optimism. In fact, it was in 1857 that the partners—M. Ticknor, E. Ticknor, and C. B. Robbins—had extended the business into St. Louis. They attributed their success to two principles: that of a policy of "live and let live—quick sales and small profits," and that of operating "strictly a cash business, selling on time to no one." They declared that "by a strict adherence to this rule they are enabled to sell goods from thirty to forty per cent cheaper than the same class of goods have sold for heretofore." The firm later set up a small manufactory in St. Louis that produced custom-made garments on the spot. Unlike the New Yorkers in the South who sent measurements to the North, where custom jobs were completed, the firm "secured the services of a number of excellent journeymen tailors, cutters, etc.," who furnished "clothing to order on the shortest possible notice."[9]

Competition in the Midwest. The hold that the New York manufacturers had upon the West was far weaker than the one they had on the South. First, other eastern cities—Philadelphia, Hartford, and especially Boston—were equally determined to supply the West with clothing. Second, the West itself entered into competition with the Eastern manufacturers and by the end of the 1850's some cities in the Midwest were well on their way to launching their own clothing industries.

An outstanding representative of Philadelphian clothiers in St. Louis was the firm of Ball, Worrall, and Milner. Its place of business, only a few doors away from Ticknor, Robbins, and Co., was at 164 North Main Street. A manufacturer of ready-made clothing and furnishings since 1845 in Philadelphia, Ball, Worrall, and Milner established its outlet in St. Louis in the mid-1850's.

The New England manufacturers were particularly heavy suppliers to the West. The Boston Board of Trade reported in 1857 that since 1851 sales of clothing "to the West have steadily increased . . . more rapidly than ever" and that "Boston is now acknowledged to produce a more desirable class of goods, and better adapted to the western trade, than any other market." It also reported that sales of clothing to the West in 1856 exceeded "the entire New England trade." Boston manufacturers claimed in 1858 that they were winning the "trade with the northern portion of the Middle States and with Missouri" away from New York City. Their "styles of goods," they said, were "preferred, as better adapted to their wants, than those of New York." The manufacturers also hopefully said that "with proper care and continued attention to the requirements of these markets, a still greater increase may be anticipated."[10] Shirts manufactured in New England were also very popular in the West, and E. A. Parker, a large Hartford shirt producer, supplied many of the bigger western wholesalers.

The other obstacle to the New York manufacturers was the vigor with which a number of western cities entered the field themselves. For example, producers in Cincinnati competed with New York clothiers in supplying cheaper garments to the South and West.

As early as 1826 Cincinnati had thirty-five tailor shops employing 132 men and 467 women and producing products valued at $172,815. During the next twenty-five years the clothing industry there grew at a tremendous rate and by 1841 the value of the clothing produced was estimated at $1,223,800. Ten years later it was valued at $1,947,500 and nearly 5,000 people were employed in the industry. In 1859 Cincinnati had forty-eight wholesale and eighty-six retail clothing establishments producing a product valued at $15,000,000. That year a contemporary noted that "within the last eight or ten years Cincinnati has been gaining a position as a great center of supply, by wholesale to the country merchants of Ohio, Indiana, Illinois, and Kentucky" and that "it is becoming very apparent to purchasers that they can deal here to greater advantage than in our eastern cities."[11]

The census report of 1860 estimated that the entire State of Ohio had 448 clothing establishments producing nearly $9,000,000 worth of clothing—more than the output of a number of eastern states, including Massachusetts and New Jersey. In 1861 Ohio claimed eight manufacturers of shirts, collars, and furnishings—more than in any other state except Connecticut, New York, and Pennsylvania.

Although the production of men's clothing in St. Louis never equaled that in Cincinnati, there were nevertheless many tailors in St. Louis as early as the beginning of the nineteenth century. Many of them, according to their public announcements, were quite skilled and had numerous years of experience both in eastern cities and abroad. That they had a standing in that growing city can be seen by their representation in the St. Louis Mechanics Exchange, which was formed by the local tradesmen in 1839.[12] A directory published some years later shows that St. Louis counted among its businessmen 111 clothiers, ninety tailors, and twelve dealers in men's furnishings.[13]

By the end of the 1850's the citizens of St. Louis were growing critical of the clothing shipped to them from New York. One consumer declared in 1858 that there was really no need to purchase the "slop-shop work . . . sent here from the eastern cities . . . whose only merit consists in its cheapness," when a superior product was being turned out by the city's own houses. In fact, one clothing concern, D. S. Thompson at 86 North Fourth Street, appeared to possess all of the attributes of a large New York house. It employed Harry Holsman, who had "not his superior as a coat cutter in the world." Holsman was superintendent of a large coat-cutting department. It also had an equally superior craftsman as overseer of the pantaloon-cutting department. In addition, it had a department solely for repairing clothing. Established in St. Louis in 1842, this firm grew steadily every year and claimed in 1858 to be "the largest house of the Mississippi and one of the largest in the United States."[14]

St. Louis was on its way to becoming independent of the New York apparel trade but total independence was still distant. The census report of 1860 showed that the entire men's clothing industry in Missouri produced clothing valued at less than $1,000,000, more than that of any other midwestern state, except Ohio and Kentucky, but not large enough to supply the rapidly growing West.

Chicago did not enter the competitive picture until late in the pre-Civil War period, but when it did it moved with amazing rapidity. The demand for tailors and cutters by 1853 was heavy and was reflected in these workers' wages, which in that day were considered high. Tailors in Chicago in the years from 1853 to 1855 were earning between $7 and $10 a week, while cutters, who were craftsmen of greater skill, were earning up to $16 a week.[15] The numerous jobbers located there were not only purchasing garments from the East but were also toying with the idea of manufacturing clothing themselves. A number began such operations in the late 1850's, but there was no great productive achievement in this area before the war. The entire State of Illinois produced a little more than $774,000 worth of clothing in 1860, less than Missouri and not enough to supply the large western trade that it entertained.

According to the census of 1860, the only midwestern state, other than Ohio, that produced an annual product valued at more than $1,000,000 was Kentucky. Moreover, all of the midwestern states combined—Ohio, Indiana, Michigan, Illinois, Wisconsin, Iowa, Minnesota, Nebraska, Missouri, and Kentucky–produced clothing valued at even less than that produced in the South.

VI

OUTFITTING THE FORTY-NINERS

It was late in 1848 when the news of the discovery of gold in California began to have a noticeable effect on the New York clothiers, but once the rush to the western gold fields began it became obvious that a new chapter had opened for the manufacturers. The need for clothing on the Pacific Coast was enormous and no city in that region of the country could satisfy the demand. The few tailors that were in San Francisco probably closed shop and rushed, shovel in hand, to dig in the Sacramento fields. Philip Hone keenly described the situation in his diary, when he wrote on December 16, 1848, that in California "the towns are deserted . . . business is neglected; houses stand empty . . . the necessaries of life cannot be obtained, and the people are starving, with their pockets full of gold."[1] Prices for labor and all kinds of commodities rose so sharply that "no man could give another a hand's turn for less than five dollars." Paying for an honest day's labor was almost impossible. "It was about as economical to throw away certain soiled articles of clothing and buy new ones," wrote one chronicler, "as to get the old ones cleaned, when people had to pay twelve to twenty dollars for the washing of each dozen of articles, large or small."[2] Throughout 1849 the prices for apparel continued to rise. Two hundred dollars was soon demanded for "a decent suit of clothes" in San Francisco and, since coins were rare, clothing was at first sold for so many pinches of gold dust. There is little wonder, then, about the story of a merchant who, upon arriving in San Francisco from New York, was in such haste to fill orders for clothing that instead of waiting for the arrival of New York fabrics to manufacture some overalls, he tore canvas from Conestoga Wagons and sails from abandoned ships in the bay.[3]

New York clothiers were not slow in taking advantage of the new opportunity. Philip Hone noted in January, 1849, that tailors and other tradesmen "are employed night and day in fitting out the adventurers." Advertisements directed at those departing for California became common in New York newspapers. M. Woolf, a shirt manufacturer at 61 Maiden Lane, was one of the first to take advantage of the new trade by announcing "shirts for California" in December, 1848. Soon Lewis and Hanford, the large wholesalers, began pushing their assortment: they declared in January, 1849, that it was "just the thing for Californians, who may be going out separately, or in companies." The firm of Daniel and J. Devlin declared in February, 1851, that it was "prepared for the largest demand for California clothing of every description."[4]

New York Clothiers and the Route to California. It was a fortunate maritime factor that enabled the New York clothing merchants to make so much of the new opportunity. Most freight in those years was hauled to San Francisco aboard clipper ships sailing southward to Cape Horn and from there northward to California ports. It has been estimated that two-thirds of those clippers were owned by New Yorkers and that even a greater portion used New York as the departure terminus. Furthermore, the steamship service that developed competing routes, such as Panama and Nicaragua, was also monopolized by New Yorkers.[5] The city, therefore, emerged as a jumping-off place for both freight and passengers embarking for California. Even merchants of neighboring cities were forced to ship clothing via New York clippers. Moreover, many probably also purchased their stocks in New York. One dry goods and clothing merchant in San Francisco instructed his partner in Philadelphia in the spring of 1851 to ship any garments he sent "by quick vessels from New York." In the following year he repeated the instructions when he wrote, "Please send me merchandise on every clipper and we will be able to make money. Send goods every two weeks. Send me goods directly through New York clipper." Later in the same letter he added, "with every clipper from New York send 5 or 6 packages."[6] Clothing merchants in New York City, therefore, stood to gain regardless of who the supplier was.

A good portion of the clothing loaded on clippers at the New York waterfront was securely packed in bales to withstand a trip that took betwen three and six months. "Bales of clothing" unloaded from vessels must have been a very common sight along the San Francisco pier in those years.[7]

Freight rates were naturally highest in the earliest days of the gold rush. But the rates for dry goods shipped to San Francisco via the Cape Horn route fell from $1.50 per cubic foot in 1850 to thirty cents per cubic foot in the mid-1850's. They remained at about that rate for the rest of the decade.[8] After 1854, however, clipper ships were used less and less in the San Francisco trade, because the shippers awoke to their many disadvantages: a good portion of the cargo was always damaged by the water that penetrated the ship's timbers, insurance rates were higher on clippers than on other vesssls, and the clippers' construction permitted only a minimum amount of freight to be handled. But they did have the one great advantage of speed, which made them indispensable in the early years when expeditious deliveries to California were of paramount importance.

Manufactures and Importations in California. Dependence upon outside sources for a supply of clothing remained strong on the Pacific Coast from the gold rush until the end of the pre-Civil War period. The few craftsmen of San Francisco, such as Lazarus Everhart, a fashionable tailor on Montgomery Street,[9] were in no position to supply the tremendous rush of orders that occurred in 1849. As the city became rapidly populated in the following years a few tailors opened shops along the main thoroughfares.[10] Considering the expense of skilled labor, any attempt at extensive operations would have been a difficult undertaking. Even in 1853, when conditions were becoming somewhat more stabilized, tailors in San Francisco were earning "at least five times higher than what was paid similar workers in Atlantic states," that is, about $4 a day. Even seamstresses were receiving between $40 and $70 plus board for each month's work.[11]

As the decade progressed, however, the number of tailor shops in San Francisco increased. There were 41 in 1858, 138 in 1860, and 154 in 1861, in which year a California clothing concern was even searching in New York City for a foreman for "a very large California clothing establishment." A local directory, however, shows that the majority of clothing firms in San Francisco were called "importers," "jobbers," and "dealers." Tailor shops and manufacturers were in the minority.[12] The census of 1860 reveals that in Oregon and California the production of clothing amounted to only $79,186, and that California, which had 11 establishments, produced $59,086 of that total.

A portion of the Pacific Coast supply came from abroad from English, French, and German merchants, who were equally aware of opportunities in merchandising and who loaded vessels and shipped them off to the Golden Gate. A "California Mania" was reported in Paris in 1850, because every newspaper in that city was filled with requests for merchandise for California. One vessel, the *City of Paris,* arrived in San Francisco in May of that year loaded with wearing apparel. Two of the passengers were Felix and Emile Verdier, merchants from Paris. No sooner did the two Frenchmen debark than they realized that they had struck gold. They immediately ordered another shipment from France. At first they sold their merchandise directly from the ship, but in the following year they opened a store on Kearney Street. The firm, which grew into one of California's leading dry goods establishments, still exists today under the name of its first home, the *City of Paris.*[13]

Advertisements of imported clothing for men were noticed daily in the San Francisco newspapers. One importer announced "13 cases English-made cord and moleskin trowsers" and "80 dozen English-made fancy colored cotton shirts" in February, 1852. Another advertised "the largest and best selected stock of clothing and furnishing goods ever imported to this country" in the same year.[14]

Apart from New York City, San Francisco was the largest receiver of imported ready-made clothing in the United States. It imported $83,411 worth from 1855 to 1856, $66,390 from 1856 to 1857, $121,933 from 1857 to 1858, $101,105 from 1858 to 1859, and $95,521 from 1859 to 1860. The imports into San Francisco even exceeded those into New York from 1857 to 1859, when the two cities accounted for nearly all of the imports into the country.

Commission Merchants and Auctioneers. Once the New York merchandise was in San Francisco, a portion of it was disposed of either through the efforts of commission merchants or under the hammer of the auctioneer. A number of large New York manufacturers, such as Lewis and Hanford and Wyman Brothers, relied upon commission merchants stationed in San Francisco and inland towns to dispose of the ready-made garments. In the first few years after the gold strike the streets of San Francisco overflowed with commission merchants announcing their latest receipts of clothing from New York. Case, Heiser and Co., commission merchants in San Francisco, announced on April 30, 1852, a list of the clothing it had just removed from the clipper *Eclipse.* The list included "fancy cashmere pants . . . colored Kentucky jean pants; cottonade pants; fancy tweed cashmere pants; [and] camblet jean pants."

After they arrived at San Francisco, whole cargoes of clothing were sometimes thrown directly into auction. With almost primitive business conditions prevailing in San Francisco in those years, selling through auction proved to be a convenient way of disposing of merchandise. Frequent fires, lack of storage space, shaky prices, and the desire of commission merchants for a rapid realization of their advances were a few of the factors that made auctions a convenient outlet. That the auctions were also popular at first can be seen by the frequent advertisements of them. As in New York and New Orleans, the day and time of each sale and a description of the clothing to be auctioned were always announced in advance. A variety of clothing of all grades and styles was auctioned in large or small lots in the streets of San Francisco. At times the commission merchants themselves, combining both tasks into one, conducted the auctions.[15]

Storekeepers, too, sometimes sold clothing at auction in order to test the demand for certain items. One merchant wrote to his partner in the East in 1851 that the corduroy pants he received were selling at $27 per dozen. "You know how it is," he added, "sometimes goods bring good prices at auct. and often they dont." This merchant, Alexander Mayer, probably reflected the growing attitude of numerous storekeepers in San Francisco when he declared, "I dont like to put any goods on auction." Everytime he did so, he claimed, he "had to take a big loss."[16]

Dissatisfaction with the auction system was growing because of "the heavy license duties laid upon auctioneers" and "the tax of sixty cents per one hundred dollars laid upon consigned goods" (goods shipped into California from any other state for sale in California). These tax provisions, which were incorporated into the California State Revenue Act of May 15, 1853, were objected to strongly by the commission merchants and auctioneers. Despite the review of the Act by the Supreme Court of California, which declared the measure constitutional in 1854, there was a widespread refusal to pay the duties. A contemporary wrote that "the law has not been enforced and there is considerable doubt whether it ever can or will be." Many consignees of the New York garments were undoubtedly involved in the protest, since the disposition of apparel through commission merchants and auctioneers had been popular in the days following the gold strike.

New York Clothiers in San Francisco. Wtih the rapid growth of San Francisco from a village of 800 people in 1848 to a city of 50,000 five years later, numerous New York clothing merchants decided that it was time to extend retail and wholesale outlets there just as they had done in the South and Midwest. The merchants probably realized that the importance of San Francisco lay not only in the fact that it was growing into a large community but also that, like New Orleans and St. Louis, it was emerging into a depot of supply for its surrounding area on the Pacific Coast. The interior towns and mining districts of California, as well as many wholesale merchants in Oregon, already depended on San Francisco for their daily necessities.

A number of clothing merchants who arrived in San Francisco responded primarily to the needs of the interior mining camps and a few of them moved temporarily into inland towns. Thomas Tobin, who was originally from Ireland, worked for a while for the New York dry goods house of Griffin and Pullman. In August, 1849, he left New York and established himself in the clothing business in San Francisco. Shortly afterward he left San Francisco to enter the dry goods business in Downieville in Sierra County. In 1853 he returned to San Francisco.[17]

The town of Marysville, which originated as a mining camp in California, soon became the place where miners went to buy their supplies. By 1851 three clothing merchants had made Marysville their home. They were Joseph S. Friedman, who ran a dry goods and clothing store, and J. and C. Levin, who were dealers in ready-made clothing. Friedman later moved to San Francisco, where he had a long career as a businessman until his death in 1885.[18]

The needs of the miners were also taken care of by a merchant named Levi Strauss, who arrived in San Francisco from New York early in 1850 and soon realized that supplying working apparel to miners was as profitable as digging for gold. Moreover, with two brothers in the dry goods business in New York, he was sure of a constant flow of material. Strauss, however, did much more than open an outlet in California; rather, he launched an enterprise far greater than the one he had left in New York. At first he traveled to Sacramento, where he examined the needs of the miners and secured orders for clothing. In 1853, together with his brothers in New York, he set up a wholesale jobbing and manufacturing concern known as Levi Strauss and Co. Maintaining his buying office in New York, he began to manufacture pants and overalls designed especially for the miners. His pants, popularly known as "Levis," eventually became as popular in the West as the lasso and Colt revolver.[19]

John H. Browning, the founder of a large New York clothing firm, also paid special attention to the needs of the miners in the early days of the gold rush. William C. Browning, recalling his father's early experience, wrote some years later that "in 1848 Mr. John H. Browning started a branch store in California, making his first shipment mostly of dry-goods, but soon changed it into clothing, mostly gray flannel shirts and trowsers for the use of the miners."

Advertisements in the California newspapers show that the majority of New York clothing manufacturers who extended outlets into San Francisco were just as eager to take advantage of the rapidly growing trade in more fashionable clothing as they were to capitalize on the needs of the miners. One New York firm, Keyes and Co.–which had one partner, Seth C. Keyes, in New York to supervise factory operations—constantly advertised in San Francisco the "black and fancy frock coats, dress and party vests" and "superfine black pants" that were sold at its store on Clay Street.

Many New Yorkers in San Francisco stressed the fact that their clothing was manufactured in their New York factories and included the finest eastern styles. "Clothing—of every kind and variety, now receiving per the recent arrivals by ships *Albert, N. B. Palmer,* and *Flying Cloud,*" was declared by two clothiers, Johnson and Canfield, in the fall of 1851. These merchants advertised "the fullest and largest assortment in this market, all of which is manufactured by ourselves, and can therefore be recommended either as regards styles, quality or fabric." Many merchants listed two addresses in their advertisements—one in San Francisco and one in New York. Mawson Brothers listed its New York address as 161 Water Street and its San Francisco location as "Jackson St., above Montgomery in a brick basement." Among the firms that stressed the regularity and frequency with which they received goods from New York was Keyes and Co., which declared in 1852 that the shipment it had just opened was merely "one of a series which will be sent by every mail steamer from the manufactory of Keyes & Co., Broadway, New York," and stressed that "the latest and most beautiful style of goods will be regularly sent to our house in San Francisco."

Dealers in shirts, who were also plentiful in San Francisco, included Charles Leighton, who had operated a retail and wholesale shirt outlet in New Orleans. As soon as the rush to the gold fields began Leighton opened a second outlet in San Francisco. In his advertisements he called the new store the "First Premium Shirt Depot" and claimed always to carry "a fresh supply of . . . New York-made shirts."

Leighton was not the only enterprising New York shirt manufacturer who decided to branch out to the West Coast. The firm of L. A. Levy and T. E. Woolf opened a store called the New York Shirt Depot. Until 1852 Levy and Woolf combined both retailing and wholesaling operations. In February of that year, however, they "relinquished the retail branch of their business" and concentrated on wholesale operations to country and local dealers. Their stock, replenished regularly via New York clipper service, was periodically listed in local newspapers. On February 12, 1852, Levy and Woolf announced receipt "per *Wild Pigeon, Trade Wind* and *Golden Gate,* direct from their manufactory in New York an elegant assortment of shirts." Later that year Levy bought out Woolf's share of the business and proceeded to run both the factory in New York and the outlet in San Francisco.

After 1852 more use was made of mail steamers arriving by way of

Panama and Nicaragua in the shipment of New York clothing. Speed was essential when delivering fashionable clothing, and small invoices could be loaded easily on mail steamers which, because of their shorter route, made the voyage to California far more rapidly than did the clippers. Keyes and Co. claimed to receive new shipments every month by mail steamer.

The popularity of the New York styles assured continuing sales to the New York dealers in San Francisco. Although the two cities were 3,000 miles apart and had no railroad to connect them, the New York tailors, from the tone of their advertisements, considered themselves not very far away from the San Francisco residents. One New York dealer, George P. Fox, constantly reminded the Pacific Coast dwellers of his New York Tailoring establishment at 333 Broadway. Other New York dealers, who recognized the importance of New York-tailored garments to the Californians, served western customers by taking measurements in San Francisco and manufacturing the garments in New York for shipment back to the West Coast. The following announcement appeared in San Francisco on May 18, 1852:

"Gentlemen will please take notice—clothing made to order–the undersigned being about to visit the City of New York . . . will be happy to receive gentlemen's orders for suits of clothing. Particular personal attention will be paid to the style, quality and manufacture of each article, and in every instance a fit guaranteed, and delivered within ninety days. Measures will be taken at the 'Gentlemen's Furnishing Emporium' 272 Montgomery Street . . ."—Albert Lockwood[20]

On the same day Keyes and Co. promised delivery for a similar service in seventy days. Such advertisements tended to emphasize the almost primitive state of the clothing industry in San Francisco and that city's extreme dependence upon New York. In fact, the dependence upon the production facilities of New York was so great that one California merchant, Abraham Colman, who decided to go into the clothing business in San Francisco, moved to New York in 1859 to establish a factory to supply his West Coast outlet.[21]

Perserverance, courage, and a spirit of adventure were the necessary attributes for any clothing merchant who wanted to survive the hectic days that followed the gold rush. Many were initially frustrated by the difficulties involved in finding storage space for stock and renting stores from which to begin operations. Because of the lack of facilities and the high rents—a large store rented for as much as $6,000 a month in 1850—and the indecisiveness in the minds of many merchants about the future state of the market, much of the selling was done at first in temporary tents, sheds, and stalls. Some merchants even took to the muddy streets with packs on their backs to peddle to passers-by.

The renting of a store was no guarantee of permanency either. Frequent and drastic fires, as well as a great deal of looting, almost made it wiser for merchants to remain street peddlers. Between December 24, 1849, and June 14, 1851, six great fires raged in the business district of San Francisco. In one of the early fires it was claimed that Jesse Seligman, a New York clothing dealer, was the only merchant whose store escaped destruction. The fires were frequently followed by newspaper notices asking for "bales of clothing" that might have been "carried away intentionally or unintentionally during the fire." A reward was usually offered for recovery.

Since fires broke out frequently, a number of merchants were reluctant to carry an extensive stock. Alexander Mayer, a dealer from Philadelphia, said in March, 1851, "I rather make 20 pr. cent less and have not so much in store and go a little safe. I cant affort to tak a brig building for $800 dolls rent." That May a fire caused Mayer considerable damage.[23] Another fire in June also affected him considerably. After he surveyed the extent of the damage he wrote this to an uncle: "It is hard for me to write you again about my Misfortune. I had on the 22nd of June a large Fire . . . and I am an Heavy looser again." He wrote that he had done everything in his power to salvage the merchandise and that he had remained in the store as long as he could, despite the spreading flames. It was only after repeated pleas from the firemen that he "thought then it is the best . . . to go out . . . Rather let them Goods Burne than my self, I know you dont want that . . ." His losses, he added, were heavy because although he managed to salvage some of his merchandise, much of it was either destroyed by the flames or stolen. "A person at home," he continued, "cannot imagin this fires what takes place Here . . . You may really believe me since I left . . . I look ten years older. In all my Days a life I have not been so down hearted as I have been for the last 6 weeks . . ."

In addition to the fires the merchants also had to cope with unstable prices, an unpredictable demand for clothing, and a generally erratic business situation. The first response to the demand for clothing after the gold strike was so enthusiastic that most merchants forgot that the well had a bottom. By 1850 San Francisco was bulging with garments. On arriving in San Francisco in February of that year Mayer had remarked that there were more cashmere trousers in San Francisco than in all of Philadelphia and that there were so many vests that it was almost impossible to sell them. He wondered why he had come to

California and advised his uncle not to ship any more goods to him. Predicting that there "will be a Great many failures here," he said that there was enough clothing stored in San Francisco to keep merchants supplied for a year. In March he noted pessimistically that business continues "very dull here at present time" and that "this year are four times as many goods here as there has been Last year." Again he told his uncle not to ship any more merchandise. A few weeks later, when he received a letter saying that overcoats had been dispatched to him, he replied that he was "very much disappointed," since "there are to many here. . . . Even boys clothing are plenty," he added.

Prices kept dropping and by September, 1850, San Francisco was in the throes of a commercial panic. Throughout the rest of that year and most of the next "bales of valuable goods were sometimes not worth their storage." News of the poor state of affairs made the shippers more cautious. As the inventories in San Francisco dwindled in the latter part of 1851, prices began to rise. In May of that year Mayer ordered shipments of fancy black cashmere pants and a large assortment of red, blue, calico, and white shirts, urging that the goods be sent "by Quick vessels from New York" because they "will fetch good prices by next fall," since "there is a great consumption of clothing in this country." Throughout 1852 shipments of clothing to San Francisco increased in response to bigger demands. Although a San Francisco newspaper reported in March of that year that the clothing "market is relieved to great extent" and that "imports will be quite adequate for the consumption," Mayer urged his uncle to "please send me merchandise on every clipper & we will be able to make money."

Since oscillations in the business conditions were characteristic of the early years of the gold rush and suppliers were 3,000 miles away, it was difficult to fit supplies accurately to demands; guesswork had to take the place of careful analysis. Thus, 1853 and the first half of 1854 comprised another period of excessive shipments. With the market completely glutted in the latter part of 1854, prices again toppled downward and a number of clipper ships were turned back to New York with their original cargo.

The New York merchants who dared to venture into the new communities on the Pacific Coast faced many risks and unstable business conditions. But by the mid-1850's they managed to establish a foothold in California, as well as in every other important commercial center in the United States.

VII

RETAILING FOR THE LOCAL TRADE

While serving an extensive external market, New York City also supplied the needs of its own residents. Retailing in a city whose population was increasing with greater rapidity than that of any other city in the Union was, or course, quite profitable. The clothing merchants quickly learned to cater to the needs of native New Yorkers.

The dramatic growth of the city's population was basic to the success of the local retail trade. A town of 60,000 people in 1800, New York City had a population of nearly 1,000,000 on the eve of the Civil War. The growth was steady, but some of the biggest increases took place between 1820 and 1860. The greatest increase occurred between 1840 and 1860, when the population grew from 312,000 to 813,000. Moreover, as early as 1830 it was estimated that the visitors who flocked daily to New York for business and pleasure numbered 20,000.[2]

New York City as a Center of Fashions. As cities grew in the nineteenth century they were sometimes noted for setting styles of behavior and dress that were imitated by surrounding towns and rural areas. And just as Paris and London set fashions throughout western Europe, New York City dictated fashions in the United States.

Although most of the South's smaller planters usually dressed shabbily in clothing that was far from what was considered correct in the eastern urban centers,[3] they preferred the New York fashions. As early as 1826 most clothing merchants, such as those in Macon, Georgia, stressed that their garments were of "the latest New York fashions." One dealer in Baton Rouge declared some years later that his store stocked New York, Paris, and London fashions, thereby placing New York before the two European capitals.[4] Moreover, the fact that the larger southern clothiers, such as Norris and Way, Montross and Stilwell, and Alfred Munroe, invited southerners to leave their measurements so that in a month or two their garments could be made in New York, reflected both the lack of southern industrialization and a preference for New York fashions.

The style leadership of New York was also recognized in midwestern and western cities. A large tailoring establishment in St. Louis advertised that it was "constantly receiving by express every new pattern as soon as it makes its appearance in the East." In San Francisco the commission merchants advertised their latest purchases from the East and emphasized that they were "the latest New York style." Even an Englishman admitted in 1830 that, although he found men's clothing somewhat more expensive in New York, "the fit and cut, however, are incomparably better than in England."[5]

The New York clothiers, well aware that they were style leaders, were at times bold and experimental in fostering fashions. In the fall of 1853 they presented the "New York Surtout," a tight-fitting topcoat of novel design. Once the clothiers realized that New York fashions had a special appeal, they made every effort to maintain the appeal by paying careful attention to style. One writer said that "a doubt might have existed as to this policy in the outset, but success *then*, has made it a necessity *now*." In 1858 the New York Chamber of Commerce reported that the clothiers had "given great attention to, and spared no expense in improving the character and style of their manufacture; so that everywhere throughout the country New York made clothing is popular over all others for the superiority of its make, and for the taste and neatness of its style." A magazine of fashion had announced in 1854 that "New York is at once the London and the Paris of the Western hemisphere, being the . . . fountain-head of the fashions," and predicted that "the day will come when this city will set the fashions for the world."

That year, however, one disgruntled observer noted in an article entitled "Tricks of Tailors" that the perpetual change of modes in New York amounted to no more than a big "trick" played by the clothiers upon the American people. The writer, who considered style-changing a quick way to make money, was convinced that tailors persuaded "half a dozen men of high fashion, who look well in anything, to parade this new invention in Broadway" to make everybody else "appear out of date."[6] Although there may have been some truth in the gripe, the fact remains that the frequent changes in styles in New York were due largely to the frequent changes abroad. Indeed, the appeal of New York's fashions lay in the fact that they closely imitated the latest London and Paris designs.[7]

Both France and England contributed greatly to the changing fashions in men's garments in the years prior to the Civil War. The movement for the long trousers began in Paris about 1800 largely as a reaction to the knee breeches worn by the aristocracy of the Old Regime. The new style, adapted in England, quickly became popular in the United States, too. England also developed a variation in the cut and introduced the "Wellington trousers." English dandies, such as the

Prince of Wales and George Bryan, who was known as Beau Brummell, also introduced changes in dress that were copied in America. Bryan was largely responsible for popularizing starched shirts, collars, and cuffs; the practice of changing shirts once a day; and the Prince Albert coat, which he wore during his visit to the United States in the spring of 1860. Peg-top trousers were brought to America from France, where they had been authorized by Louis Napoleon for the French army.

Social changes, such as a growing urban business and professional class, and the new means of transportation by steam also hastened changes in costume. The swallow-tailed coat became fashionable and black and brown suits were worn because they did not show the dust, smoke, and soot produced by the new means of travel. Vests remained flashy in both appearance and design.[8]

Many of those changes were introduced in Europe and quickly copied in New York. "The dress of the people differs little from our own," wrote one English visitor in 1828. Another found in 1829 that "the gentlemen savoured rather more of Paris than London." A visitor 20 years later remarked that New York gentlemen in general smacked "*a la Francaise*" and that "looking merely to the people, you might often fancy yourself in the Boulevards, instead of in Broadway."[9]

It was also noticed that a number of New Yorkers made it a habit to purchase garments from London tailors, whom they preferred to the New York craftsmen. London tailors, in fact, advertised regularly in New York newspapers, just as the New York tailors advertised in the southern and western publications. With steamers shuttling constantly back and forth across the Atlantic, New York felt as close to London as it did to New Orleans and Charleston. "Aristocracy versus Democracy," announced one London tailor in the *New York Herald* in 1840. "Gentlemen inclined to go ahead in the Atlantic steamers, will do well to call at Rolfe & Co.'s Merchant Tailors No. 35 Great Marlborough Street, Regent Street London . . . being assured by Rolfe & Co. of the first style of fashion." In 1851 the same newspaper carried advertisements of six other London clothiers.[10]

Immigrant tailors in New York announced in their advertisements that they had practiced their craft abroad in the hopes of increasing business. John Ditchet advertised in 1807 "that he arrived from *Europe* about three years last" and that "prior to the above specified time the said J. D. had eleven years practice in the art of cutting." Thomas Stokes, a merchant tailor on William Street, prided himself on having originally been a tailor in London. M. Jeffery of 257 Broadway boasted of a similar background a few years later.[11] John Clark described himself in 1834 as a tailor "from Bond St. London . . . ready to fit gentlemen in the most elegant fashion." W. J. Jacob, a merchant tailor at 40 Fulton Street, declared that he was originally "from the house of Stultz, London."

Newcomers from France, too, took pains to make a special point of their country of origin. In 1825 A. Arnoux printed his advertisements entirely in French. Another craftsman described himself as "Mr. Becker, tailor, from Paris." Although Shafer and Co., Broadway clothiers, were not Frenchmen, they nevertheless tried to impress their customers in 1846 with the fact that they had "concluded a permanent arrangement, as cutter, with Mr. P. Andriot, late of Rue Castiglione, Paris, well known to most of our fashionables who have visited Europe."

Since London and Paris were acclaimed as the centers from which correctness in fashion emanated, many New York clothiers emphasized the fact that their stock originated from those two cities. Thomas Stokes announced in 1809 that he had "commenced an arrangement to receive regularly the Fashions prevailing at the West End of London." The Wall Street clothing firm of R. Calrow and Co. declared in 1822 that it had "just received by the *Cincinnatus,* from Messrs. Stultz & Co. gentlemen's very late *London Fall Fashions,* of an entire new model."[12] In 1838 John Bate announced that he received "London and Paris Fashions . . . monthly." Ellis and Bancker, merchant tailors, declared in 1841 that "London and Paris fashions will be regularly received." In the same year Arthur L. Levy informed his patrons that he kept "an agent in London and Paris" so that no change in style could escape him. T. M. Fretz, who occasionally traveled abroad to discover the latest fashions, always informed his customers of his return.

In the late 1820's New York City began to publish weekly and monthly periodicals of fashion. One of the earliest, *Le Mirroir du Beau Monde,* was scheduled to appear weekly in the summer of 1829 and was said to be "embellished . . . with coloured plates of fashions in dress, accompanied with explanatory remarks and general observation . . ." *The Quarterly Reports of London and Paris Fashions,* published by Williams and Sons in 1834 at $5 a copy, promised to include "every change of fashion."[13] The New York daily newspapers also began to include comments on the latest fashions. For example, the *New York Herald,* on January 15, 1839, published a report on "London and Paris Fashions for January." In a related development, a number of custom tailors, such as T. Oliver and E. H. Maxwell, branched away from their craft and became fashion reporters. Oliver wrote in 1840 "that he has visited Europe for the purpose of reporting the English and French Fashions, and is now getting up a Plate for the spring and summer." He also said "that his acquaintance with nearly all the fashionable tailors of London, will afford him every facility for obtaining the earliest and most correct information with regard to any change of fashion." Oliver continued to publish his own semiannual reports throughout the following decade. Meanwhile, Maxwell, a tailor and dealer in tailors' goods, declared in 1844 that he was "the only agent in America for the elegant French Journals of Fashion, published monthly in Paris."

The New York fashion reporters probably did as much as anyone else in raising the standards of American dress, in creating a consciousness of proper attire, and in enhancing the reputation of the city as the retail center for men's clothing. Genio C. Scott's *The Mirror of Fashion* constantly advocated improved dressing habits for the American male. The publication first appeared in 1840 and sold to subscribers at $2 per year. In 1853 it was enlarged, and it became a kind of primer of dress for men to follow. Scott, a self-appointed teacher, attempted to instruct the average male in the improvement of his appearance. He considered "dress, which invests and decorates the body . . . not less one of the fine arts than architecture. . . ." He also believed that America need not fear, nor attempt to stem, "the tide of foreign dictation which governs our personal appearance"; rather, he said, Americans must modify what they receive to conform to their way of life. "In this country," he wrote, "where we have no classes above laboring, it is necessary that the dress shall not check or impede the free use of the limbs." While he believed that dress should be "something with everyone," he warned against its becoming "everything with some." Scott was pleased to note in 1855 that "more philosophy is taking possession of the customers; and persons who have hitherto . . . neglected their persons for large operations in the chase after the 'almighty dollar,'" were paying more attention to proper dress.[14]

Each month the columns of *The Mirror of Fashion* detailed what was proper to wear. In the winter of 1854 it noted "that it is now regarded as being in good taste to wear a vest and pantaloons of the same material."[15] In the fall of 1855 it said that "it is not yet time for heavy beaver cloths and fur linings, and save for riding wear, thick and warm lined over-garments are not worn. Even the beautiful New York surtout does not yet grace Broadway; but the loose cloak-coat of thin broad cloth, and the mixed sack of light cashmere, are now the favorite over-garments of this metropolis of taste and commerce."[29]

Scott claimed the honor of being the only American to hold membership in the French "Société Philanthropique of the Decorative Art," a group composed largely of leading "painters, tailors, architects . . . saddlers, harness-makers, [and] shoemakers" who sat once each year to decide which fashions would be introduced into French society.

Custom Tailors and Dealers in Ready-Made Clothing. Throughout the first half of the nineteenth century the leading retailers of men's fashionable clothing were the custom tailors. New York abounded with these craftsmen, who—as was noted by an Englishman in 1817—usually referred to themselves as merchant tailors "in conformity with the accustomed vanity of the country," rather than as tailors. Aside from the dealers in second-hand clothing, the merchant tailors were the prime source of garments before the late 1820's. After that date the tailors became the main outlet for fashionable clothes, a position they retained throughout the first half of that century.

Most of the custom tailors' advertisements included both a list of the clothes available for sale and a promise that the cut and workmanship of all finished garments would be of the highest order and that all labor would be executed by either the proprietor himself or his skilled assistants. The outstanding development in the clothing industry in the early 1800's was the introduction and general acceptance of ready-made garments. Indeed, no vast wholesale operation could have been possible without that universal acceptance. Still more important, however, was the fact that ready-made clothing was also available and popular in the fashionable urban retail trade.

Ready-made garments were not unheard of before the nineteenth century, but they were uncommon. Master tailors in London stocked ready-made clothing as early as 1681 and in the colonies a woman in Northfield, Massachusetts, made and sold shirts and breeches to the Indians in 1725.[16] In Manhattan in 1754 Jacob Reed, who operated a clothing store on William Street, sold ready-made clothing for boys and men, and in 1796 there were four "slop stores" in New York.[17]

The terms "slop stores" and "slop shops" give some idea of the regard with which ready-made clothing was held at the opening of the nineteenth century. Such establishments were used only by those who either had little concern for size and fit or placed a premium upon a quick change. Seamen and travelers, for example, patronized those shops. A New Yorker wrote that in the second decade of the nineteenth century there were only about two "slop tailors" in the city; "that is," he explained, "stores where one could purchase an outfit of garments, designed for the convenience of seamen, boatmen, and longshoremen.[18] It was generally recognized that the only ready-made clothing sold in those days was this "slop clothing" designed for those who could not "endure the delay of being measured by a tailor." Indeed, it was largely the inconvenience of a delay and the recognition of "the advantages of procuring a wardrobe at a moment's notice" that increased the popularity of ready-to-wear clothing.[19]

The movement toward ready-made clothes was confined neither to the U.S. nor to New York; rather, it was universal. An Englishman visiting New York in 1817 was surprised to discover "ready-made clothes' shops, as in London, at which articles of a cheaper but inferior description are sold." In Paris, a low-grade variety of ready-made clothing was manufactured and sold as early as the late 1820's. Philadelphia, meanwhile, had been retailing ready-made appearel since the start of that decade. It was in that city in 1824 that twenty-one-year-old Jacob Reed ended his tailor's apprenticeship and commenced to retail ready-made garments on his own account. His firm is known today as one of Philadelphia's larger clothiers, Jacob Reed Son's.[20]

It is quite possible that without America's democratic system the retail market for ready-made clothing would not have expanded so rapidly as it did. Moreover, because the American mind lent itself so well to the production of interchangeable and uniform products, it was possible to popularize a product with few individual differences. For these and other reasons, in no country did the ready-made clothing movement spread with such rapidity as it did in the United States. "In styles of clothing," wrote one observer, "we are generally content to receive instructions from Paris, but we doubt whether the Parisians ever dreamed of costumes for the millions as that which has been developed in America."[21] Despite the claim of one British clothing firm that 80% of all Englishmen were purchasing ready-made garments by 1860, and despite the claim that E. Moses and Son was manufacturing "ready-made suits that a Beau Brummel would have been proud to wear, at prices that a mechanic could afford to pay,"[22] Britons had considerable contempt for the ready-made suit long after it had become popular in America. One of England's leading designers, Henry Wampen, wrote in 1863 that "ready-made articles of apparel . . . find their admittance only among the vulgar, or those devoid of taste." Only "in countries where people are sunk below the standard of taste, or have perhaps never reached it . . . ready-made clothes establishments are to be found; and that in the same degree that people advance in culture of taste, order trades . . . increase, and those of the opposite kind decrease," he said, adding "that in every town upon the globe among the higher classes there are order trades; and amongst those void of taste and the poor, there are ready-made establishments."[23]

Criticism of the workmanship of ready-made garments was found in the United States, too, but it was never so severe. Even the strongest opponents admitted by 1860 that there were two grades of slop work—"the cheap . . . and that of the best quality," and that a large house, although it stocked "heavy lines of the medium and lower grade . . .is obliged also to keep a full assortment of fine goods, equal in every respect to the very best custom-made work."

One factor that helped the ready-made clothing movement to spread so freely in America was the absence of social barriers that forbid one class to wear the clothing of another. Visitors from abroad often remarked upon the fine appearance of "even American laborers." James Stuart, an Englishman who visited New York in 1828, was captured by the "easy and less artificial manners in the mass of the people" and considered it a novelty to discover "the immense number of people of colour—many of them as well dressed as the whites." Another visitor, James Boardman, remarked that "the carters, workmen, and others, who earn their bread by the sweat of their brow, appeared extremely well clothed." Still another visitor noted that all "articles of clothing are . . . at the command of the lowest members of society, which, but a century since, were scarcely within the reach of crowned heads." In 1853 Horace Greeley said that "no distinction of clothing between gentlemen and otherwise can be seen in the United States, as was true of Europe." Here, he said, "every sober mechanic has his one or two suits of broadcloth, and, so far as mere clothes go, can make as good a display, when he chooses, as what are called the upper classes."[24] It was said that America's rural inhabitants, too, were dressed much more fashionably than were their European counterparts. One observer wrote that French and German emigrants poured daily into New York harbor "hatless, bonnetless and shoeless . . . and if by chance a broadcloth coat is to be discerned in the company, it carries on its face and in its cut the evidence of the days of Charlemagne or William the Conquerer."

The custom tailors quickly entered the field of ready-made garments by dividing their shops into separate departments for order work and for ready-to-wear clothes. Prior to 1835 most of those tailors stressed their fashionable custom work in their advertisements and delegated the ready-made garments to the bottom of the announcements. After that, however, the stress was placed on the ready-made garments, which were described more and more frequently at the top of the advertisements.

Only a few tailors had emphasized the ready-made garments in the early 1820's. Samuel Whitmarsh, a "Draper & Tailor" located at 116 Broadway in a two-story building opposite the then fashionable City Hotel, used the upper floor for custom sales and the lower floor for the storage of ready-made garments. In May 1825 Whitmarsh announced that he had "constantly on hand, a splendid collection of goods in his line, comprising an assortment of every new and fashionable article in the market, which will be made to order in the first style at short notice." He added that "for the accommodation of Gentlemen traveling, others who, in cases of emergency may wish genteel garments, ready made, he will keep a choice assortment constantly on hand, made of the best materials, and in every respect the same as those made to measure." James A. Campfield, who operated a "Boys Clothing Emporium" at 303 Broadway, kept "a constant supply of ready-made dresses, for boys of any age, of the latest and most fashionable pattern, to suit the different tastes of parents." Campfield, who was originally a custom tailor, also never failed to mention his "clothing for Gentlemen . . . made to order at the shortest notice."

Sometimes the custom tailors included in their stocks of ready-made garments articles of custom-made apparel that had been rejected by their patrons, or clothing that had been ordered and never picked up. J. Major advertised in 1839 "a lot of superfine coats, ordered during the past year and not called for." After 1835 many of the tailors united their sales of ready-made clothing with their order trade, and after 1840 their advertisements emphasized ready-made clothing and merely mentioned the custom work. Jacob Vanderbilt advertised in 1847 that he had on hand a few thousand ready-made garments and "more than five hundred pieces of fashionable goods, which will be made to order in a style of elegance." That year Francis H. McElroy said that at his new establishment at 234 Broadway he would "at all times . . . have on hand the best and most fashionable of ready made garments, and will attend punctually to any custom work." In 1847 G. B. Clarke advertised ready-made summer suits, mentioning at the bottom of the announcement that "these articles are sold in addition to my legitimate business of making clothes of any description to order." By 1851 even Brooks Brothers placed more emphasis on ready-made clothing than on its "Merchant Tailoring" department, which had been the cornerstone of its business. In the 1850's James Little and Co., merchant tailors at 412 Broadway, advertised "the most elegant, neat fitting, well made and durable garments . . . [and] goods also made to order at the shortest notice."

The increasing popularity of ready-made garments forced the custom tailor not only to include a substantial supply of such apparel in his shop but also to alter the manner of his traditional service. Speed in the order trade had become all-important. In 1838 one tailor advertised "whole suits made, if requested, in 12 hours." Another, Edward Fox, boasted in 1843 that he could make a whole suit of clothing in a few hours. J. C. Booth and Co. in 1845 promised "full suits furnished at a few hours notice."[25]

The custom tailoring business, which had emphasized craftsmanship, was badly shaken by the 1850's. Many worked in both retailing and tailoring, while others abandoned tailoring completely to turn exclusively to retailing. Still others sold their shops altogether and sought new employment.

Nevertheless, the custom tailor did not lose his place in American society. He was still a most important figure in the industry, although he had been transformed from a craftsman who took a month to cut a coat to one who emphasized speed. And he still remained prosperous. In 1860 a survey of the custom trade in Philadelphia, a city similar in nature to New York, showed "that certain customer houses here do a larger and more profitable business than any tailoring establishment of the period before the commencement of the wholesale manufacture. With the increase of aristocratic refinement and the cultivation of taste in dress, the masters of the customer's mystery have endeavored to keep pace, and the result is, that they enjoy a kind of patronage which those who manufacture for the masses cannot hope to gain. The old tailor 'shops' of our fathers have given place to palatial stores, in which the fashionable gentlemen may lounge, look over the latest styles of goods, select patterns and give orders, with exquisite satisfaction."[26]

Ready-Made Clothing for Boys. There were probably no boys' ready-to-wear clothing establishments in New York prior to 1820. Moreover, the prices charged by custom tailors for boys' garments were quite high. As a result, such clothing was made at home either by a seamstress or by the household mistress from, as one New Yorker described them, "the discarded garments of father or elder brother." During the 1820's, however, two dealers entered the specialty field of boys' clothing. One, James A. Campfield, operated a children's clothing store in 1824. The other, Charles Herwick, had a boys' clothing store at 408 Broadway in 1827. Herwick claimed to "keep constantly on hand a large and general assortment of boy's clothing of the greatest variety and of very latest fashions." Although both dealers also handled clothing for men, their advertisements stressed the stock for boys.

As the years passed boys' clothing became an important branch of the ready-made clothing field. *The Mirror of Fashion* reported in 1854 that "the numerous extensive establishments" of boys' clothing "that now add to the beauty of our city" are proof of the "very great trade . . . in children's clothing," and promised to devote more of its pages to children's wear in the future. By 1856 a city directory listed five firms that dealt exclusively in boys' clothing, and by 1861 it listed six such firms.[27] In addition, many retailers of men's garments devoted a section of their stores, or at times an entire showroom, to juvenile attire. In 1845 George T. Green, a large dealer on Chatham Street, described himself as a "dealer in Mens, boys, & children clothing." Ten years later Rogers and Co., a huge establishment at the corner of Fulton and Nassau streets, devoted an entire showroom to the display of boys' clothing and claimed that "never has such a variety of boy's fall and winter clothing been offered in any New York establishment."

Retailing by Mail. A service offered by New York clothiers to customers in distant parts of the country was that of filling mail orders for clothing. The custom tailors, who were the first to add ready-made garments to their stocks, were also the first to go into the mail-order business. Samuel Whitmarsh, a Broadway custom tailor, advertised in 1825 that "persons at a distance, by sending the height and size round the breast and waist, in inches, can be furnished with complete suits, warranted to fit." J. Burke and Co. said in 1837 that "orders from abroad [would be] strictly attended to, and neatly packed and sent to any part of the United States." Charles Herwick, proprietor of the Boys' Clothing Store, said that if any of his garments did not fit, he would gladly refund the customer's money, provided that the clothing was returned within two weeks.

A few of the larger firms, such as Devlin and Co., which did a retail as well as a wholesale business, probably offered their distant customers printed instructions concerning the taking of measurements before ordering by mail. In addition, they might also have mailed price lists periodically to their customers. By the end of the first half of the century a large house could keep quite busy filling mail orders. In 1860 Brooks Brothers supplied clothing by mail to customers in Pittsfield, Massachusetts, and Louisville, Kentucky.[28]

Retail Prices. Most retail sales in the numerous shops along Broadway, Chatham Street, Fulton Street, the Bowery, and adjoining thoroughfares were done across the counter. After the early 1830's a small number of custom tailors and dealers in ready-made clothing advertised their prices. As a result, it is possible to have an idea about the cost of men's clothing between 1830 and 1861. The cost picture, however, cannot be accurate, because the majority of the clothiers did not list prices and the few who did probably engaged in the price-bargaining that prevailed in both retail and wholesale transactions. Moreover, the leading firms seldom, if ever, listed their prices, and it is also possible that the prices that were announced were not characteristic of the true state of affairs. Folwell and Brevoort, clothiers in 1840, said, "We forebear giving to the public our bill of fare, after the manner of the numerous third rate establishments, who puff themselves into a brief existence like the vendors of patent medicines."[29]

Some advertisements also did not make it clear as to whether the prices they listed were for custom or for ready-made garments. Furthermore, the prices told little of the quality and workmanship of the garments involved. Finally, the price listings prior to 1844 were generally for custom-made garments, while those after 1844 were usually for ready-made garments.

The general trend of wholesale prices in New York from 1834 to 1862 further complicates the cost picture. An inflationary period from 1834 to 1836 was followed by seven lean years, when prices dropped 34 per cent. A gradual recovery from 1843 to 1847 was succeeded by a drop in 1848. Prices then rose gradually and steadily, reached a peak in 1857, dropped tremendously in 1858, and remained low until the war prosperity began in 1862.[30]

Bearing in mind these barriers to a true picture of retail prices, let us study some prices noted from 1838 to 1844 in advertisements in the *New York Herald*. In those years the custom tailors charged prices that ranged as follows:[31]

Year	*Overcoats*	*Coats*	*Pants*	*Vests*
1838	$20 to $30	$12 to $31	$5 to $10	$2 to $6
1839	14 " 35	12 " 31	4 " 12	1 " 8
1840	17 " 27	14 " 32	4 " 12	3 " 6
1841	17 " 27	14 " 32	5 " 10	2 " 6
1842	10 " 30	12 " 24	5 " 10	7 " 9
1843	10 " 30	16 " 24	5 " 7	2 " 4
1844	10 " 30	12 " 22	3 " 8	2 " 4

In many of their advertisements the custom tailors listed separate prices for work done for customers who supplied their own fabrics.

These charges for the same years ranged from $6.75 to $10.50 for overcoats in 1838 to $1 to $1.75 for vests in 1844.[32] Dealers in ready-made clothing occasionally announced prices which ranged from $3 to $17 for overcoats in 1845 to $1 to $8 for pants in 1860.[33]

An entire suit of clothing—that is, coat, pants, and vest—was rarely advertised as a unit before 1845. Rather, individual prices were listed. There were, however, some places where a "suit" of clothing could be bought before 1845. In 1833 one clothier advertised "that he is now ready to furnish a suit of clothes made of the finest Saxony cloths" at $25 a suit, provided that the customer would arrange to take four suits each year and to return the old ones at the end of the year. One desperate buyer advertised in 1836 that he "wanted immediately two or three suits of clothes, comprising in each, a coat, pantaloons and vest, of fashionable materials and make, for which cash on the counter will be paid down." But such occurrences were rare.[34]

By the mid-1840's, however, a few dealers in ready-made clothing were listing prices for suits. In 1845 D. Owen's Clothing Store sold a suit for $14. In 1847 two firms advertised summer suits ranging in price from $3 to $25. In 1849. a "Five Dollar Suit Store" opened on the corner of Beekman and Nassau Streets. In February of the following year the store's proprietors advertised that their "$5 suits are the most elegant, the neatest, and the cheapest style of Spring Clothing ever offered to the dear public. They consist of cloth coat, cashmere pants, and fancy vest." Sales of suits increased steadily and became more and more popular. "Complete business suits" were advertised in 1859 by Evans, a large Fulton Street retailer, at prices ranging from $6 to $20. Rogers and Raymonds, another Fulton Street dealer, sold suits in its boys' department at $3.50.

In studying the prices for male apparel listed in the advertisements, this fact becomes clear: the prices for ready-made clothing were far closer to the reach of the average consumer than were the prices of the clothing previously produced for the custom trade. Moreover, since—in the above tabulations—the prices of the custom tailor were generally in a period of falling prices and the prices of the retailer of ready-made clothing were generally in a period of rising prices, the difference is ever more appreciable. In addition, because his prices were so high, the custom tailor was in a poor position to satisfy the retail needs of New York. The high prices were noticed even by English travelers, some of whom noted that costs here exceeded those in England by from 25 to 50%.[35]

By the time of the Civil War it was generally recognized that the outstanding achievement of ready-made clothing was "the reduction of prices which it has occasioned in what may be justly regarded as one of the first necessities of man." It is certainly likely that the pressure of the low-priced ready-made articles forced many of the custom dealers to lower their prices, too. In 1858, a year of very low prices, one retailer declared that his shop was the "only place in the city where garments are made to order at the same price as ready made."

Rents and Locations. By 1830 the principal retailers of men's clothing were located on Broadway, Greenwich Street, Canal Street, Chatham Street, and the Bowery. Broadway, below Canal Street, was the main center of fashion, and few travelers visiting New York failed to comment on the thoroughfare's "large commodious shops of every description." As early as 1807 Broadway had been called "the Bond Street of London." In 1833 it was compared "with Regent's Street in London, the Corso in Rome, and the Strado Toledo at Naples"; two years later its stores were said to be as "elegant and richly stocked as any in London"; and in 1844 it was described as "the greatest mart for the sale of gentlemen's wearing apparel in the United States."[36]

Broadway was also a street of hotels, a fact not overlooked by the numerous retailers who rented space for their shops on the hotels' ground floors in order to secure the trade of the travelers and tourists, as well as of the New Yorkers.[37] Among the hotels used by the retailers were the famous City Hotel at the start of the nineteenth century and the Astor House and the St. Nicholas Hotel which, in the 1850's, housed such clothiers as Alfred Munroe and George T. Green.

Rents and land values, which were enormous in the city's retail area, constituted an obstacle to the clothiers, many of whom were not so fortunate as Henry S. Brooks, who in 1818 was able to buy for $15,250 the ground and building for his first shop. By 1832 the space for a store with a frontage of 25 feet and a width of 100 feet in one of the leading shopping centers brought $20,000 and more. That year "a small piece of ground, which possessed the advantage of three frontages," was sold for $140,000.[38] Thus, the retailer faced the alternative of either moving northward and being excluded from the commercial center of lower Manhattan or remaining and facing the expense of a high yearly rental. In 1836 rents " in the lower part of the City" were said to be "exceeded in price, by no area of equal dimensions in England—perhaps not in the World." Moreover, competition for the limited space below City Hall served "to raise the price of land to an extravagant height" and by 1845 even a small unfurnished store was rented for $1,000 a year.[39]

Broadway commanded the highest rentals in the area. By 1835 the rents for its stores ranged "from 6,000 to 10,000 dollars a year." As a result, according to the *New York Herald* in 1843, "purchasers on Broadway are obliged to pay more for an article of dress than elsewhere." As a further result, a number of more economical, but perhaps less fashionable, retailers opened shops on a street running parallel to Broadway—the Bowery. Charles Dickens, during his visit to New York in 1842, observed that there "the stores are poorer . . . the passengers less gay" and the "clothes ready made." By 1849 the Bowery was "the leading area to buy ready made clothing" and "a man [was] a perfect green-horn who would think of going anywhere else to spend his money." A shopper entering a store "at the corner of Walker Street and the Bowery" remarked in amazement at the "forests of pantaloons . . . oceans of waistcoats . . . [and] plantations of faultless coats" and complained of the "difficulty . . . encountered . . . in making a choice from such a superabundance of elegance." The same shopper, who called the prices "very reasonable both for suits for men and boys," noted that there were numerous similar establishments along the Bowery.

The stores on the Bowery, which were not so elegant as those on Broadway, had open fronts and protective awnings that gave the impression that the entire street was one long store. And the prices were so low that a visitor from South Carolina noticed in 1851 that "everything can be bought 15 or 20 per cent cheaper than in Broadway, and equally fine in appearance, and as good in quality," although "the pattern and style may be a little different."[40] The Bowery clothiers agreed that the savings they passed on to the consumers were due directly to their not being on Broadway. One merchant moved from Broadway and immediately lowered his prices 10 per cent. The Baldwin Clothing Establishment at 70-72 Bowery claimed a savings of $40,000 . . . yearly by being off Broadway." It was even said that the lower rents and prices, as well as "the pushing retail trade," on the Bowery,[41] helped to popularize ready-made clothing.

Chatham Street was the third center of ready-made garments. One observer said of it that "on the right-hand it seems that every house is a ready-made clothing establishment." Chatham Street, however, suffered from being a center of second-hand apparel, too.

Advertising. Newspaper advertising was in its infancy in the years before the Civil War and, although the New York clothiers made ample use of the columns of the city's newspapers, their notices were generally dull and uninspiring. One retailer with thirty years of experience said that "there is nothing in the reading line so 'flat, stale and unprofitable' as the advertising pages of our newspapers" and that each advertiser must have "taken the greatest care to eliminate every original illustration of his idea from his advertisement."[42] Only on a rare occasion did an advertisement contain a note of originality. For example, Edward McCollum, inspired poetically in 1838 in the *New York Herald,* publicized himself with a jingle, part of which follows:

"On a system entirely his own
He cuts clothes for gentlemen and boys
And makes them as well, will be shown,
For workmen the best he employs . . .

"Pantaloons finely cut to the form
That will also be worn with ease,
Fit for weather that's chilly or warm
And which he will warrant to please."[43]

Brooks Brothers also took occasional plunges into poetry. "Fly at once to Brooks Brothers," it urged in 1859, for there

"They best can assist you to bear out your plan
For they either have got or will speedily make you
The best suit of clothes ever seen upon man."[44]

In 1850 P. L. Rogers advertised thusly: "Room, boys Room! there is plenty of room in the extensive wholesale and retail clothing store of our friend P. L. Rogers, 76 Fulton Street." There was a similar determination to sell in this announcement: " 'Fits' that are 'Fits'—if you want 'Fits'—that is a good fitting coat, vest, or pantaloons, drop in and see Billy Muir . . . 208 Broadway." This burst of erudition came from a Cortland Street merchant in 1853: "The apparel oft proclaims the man, for so says Shakespeare and so says H. L. Foster, wholesale and retail clothiers." There was a note of warning in this advertisement of Edward T. Hackett in 1854: "A marked man is he who wears clothing from the Emporium of Hackett . . . for his garments cannot be surpassed."[45]

Poor poetry and occasional misuses of famous quotations were about the only original items in the newspaper advertising of the clothiers. On the other hand, the advertising in the various city directories was interesting and often imaginative. Covering a full page at times, the advertisements occasionally included sketches of the stores and the streets on which they were located.

However, only a minority of the retailers ever engaged in advertising at all, because they had not yet grasped its importance. Samuel H. Terry, a severe critic of advertising, believed that advertising should be confined to special occasions "when a business is newly commenced, or upon the occurrence of any notable event, as an arrival of a renewed supply of articles . . . the receipt of some special article which has been scarce . . . or a general reduction in the price of many articles, as sometimes occurs towards the close of a season."

The retailers did, however, advertise on their own premises. Tourists during and after the late 1830's constantly remarked about the numerous placards, signs, and outdoor advertisements of the New York merchants. One visitor in 1837 noticed that along Broadway he could not turn his head without seeing one display or another. The merchants, he wrote, had even provided for those who walk with their eyes to the ground "by having large marble tablets, like horizontal tomb-stones, let into the flag pavements . . . in front of their shops, on which is engraven in duplicate turning both ways, their names and business."[46] Another tourist remarked in 1845 that "every house in the business part of the city is plastered over with enormous letters, from the basement to the attics, with the names and callings of the fifty different people that dwell therein." Still another observed some of the shopkeepers had suspended large painted signs across the gutters between supporting beams planted on either side. Some ready-made clothing dealers even hung their merchandise outside their stores during business hours, so that "the coat-tails and pantaloons . . . flap about the face of the pedestrian, like the low branches in a woodpath."

Retail Establishments. The physical appearance of New York's retail stores attracted little praise in the years prior to 1815; after that date, however, some people did laud the size of the stores. One Englishman remarked in 1817 that "the shops (or stores, as they are called) have nothing in their exterior to recommend them; there is not even an attempt at tasteful display. The linen and woolen drapers . . . leave quantities of their goods loose on boxes in the street, without any precaution against theft."[47] Another visitor "accustomed to the splendour of display in Regent Street, or Oxford Road," found retail stores on Broadway in 1833 "deficient in external attractions." Francis J. Grund, an Englishman who visited New York in 1835, thought that the retailers exhibited "less taste in the display of their goods than either the French or the English" because of the habits of economy so storngly embedded in the character of the American consumer, who was always suspicious of too fancy a display and who valued "merchandise only according to its intrinsic worth and usefulness."[48] Ten years later the shops were described as "very second-rate affairs, there not being in the whole city half-a-dozen that have not pretensions to elegance or taste." In 1850, according to one observer, most of the stores were small, crowded, too hot in the summer, poorly heated in the winter, and dismally lighted all year around, and featured few window displays.[49]

Not all observers, however, were critical of the appearance of the stores, and some even praised it. In 1828 James Stuart found signs more neatly painted here than they were in England. In 1836 Felton remarked that "plates of the newest London fashions" were "displayed in the shop windows of every tailor in New York." A year later Frederick Marryat noticed that many of the stores had "already been fitted up with large plate-glass fronts, similar to those in London." Francis Wyse said in 1845 that the stores were "generally commodious, tolerably well supplied, and tastefully fitted up" and that they would "do credit to any of the fashionable thoroughfares of Bath, London, or elsewhere."

As the movement for ready-made clothing gained momentum, showrooms were expanded to display larger stocks. In the spring of 1847 Jacob Vanderbilt, who was located at 36 Maiden Lane, featured "over five thousand ready made garments." Three years later Michael Conaway included in his "immense stock of fashionable ready made clothing . . . 1,000 coats . . . 5,000 vests . . . 5,000 pants." In 1853 the Broadway Clothing Store stocked 3,000 coats and 3,000 vests and Drumgold and Proch at 215 Broadway carried 3,000 summer pants and 1,000 Alpaca coats.[50]

During and after the late 1840's the size of the New York establishments elicited much surprise and astonishment. In 1849 the new Brooks building was called a "magnificent building." William Chambers, who visited New York in 1853, was amazed at the "size and grandeur" of some of the dry goods and clothing establishments along Broadway, some of which rose "to a height of five or six stories, with a frontage of 150 to 300 feet, and [were] built in an ornamental style of architecture." Chambers considered "these edifices . . . more like the palaces of Kings than places for the transaction of business." The following year an Englishman said that although the stores' window displays were poor their "interiors are spacious," and that "an American store is generally a very extensive apartment, handsomely decorated, the roof frequently supported on marble pillars."[51] The census report of 1860 called the clothing houses "palatial establishments . . . rivalling in extent and completeness those of any other branch of trade." Visitors who arrived in New York shortly after the start of the Civil War were amazed at the "Pompeian clothing establishments." One traveler wrote that "New York is their [the tailor shops'] fairyland—many eminent examples among them resembling, in size and elegance, rather a European palace than a republican place of traffic."[52]

Lighting a showroom so that the fabrics and clothing could be seen at their best advantage was a problem to the retailers, since electric lighting had not yet arrived. Natural light, which entered the room with different intensities and from different angles at different parts of the day, must have been a constant concern to the merchants. As a result, the retailers sometimes erred " in endeavoring to modify the light of their warerooms by shutting too much of it out, and making their places too dark," and the customer either bought his goods "half unseen" or held "them up to the light of window or door . . . and thus all the advantage which was anticipated by darkening the store, is more than lost, as the goods are seen in one of the worst lights they could have been shown in."[53] One Philadelphia clothier built his main showrooms directly under an "enormous skylight," but he was a rarity. Most of the display rooms were far too dark.

Salesmen and Clerks. The clothing salesman had achieved a professional status among the retailers by the early 1830's. One New Yorker claimed in 1835 to have been employed "in that capacity for several years."

Throughout the following years numerous requests appeared in the city's newspapers for salesmen acquainted with the retail clothing business; and since many of the retail establishments were operated either as custom tailors' shops or as outlets for ready-made garments, the salesmen were expected to be skilled cutters, too, and to work in that area when not attending to customers. Moreover, the customers probably preferred to be fitted by men who were able to cut and alter the garments they sold. Further, the salesmen were better able to close sales if, during the negotiatons, they could fit, measure, and function ably as tailors. Finally, during the slack midwinter and summer seasons, the employers liked their salesmen to work at the cutting tables on the next season's supply. As a result, many of the advertisements for salesmen required that the applicants have at least "some knowledge of cutting" and that they be able to act as foremen of small shops or "to fill any department in the above line." More important, however, was the amount of trade the salesmen could muster, and most were hired on the basis of the "set of customers, which will follow." For this reason, many salesmen seeking positions boasted of the "good share of custom" they could bring.

Despite their skills, however, the salesmen had not yet developed a polished sales technique. Thus, the complaints about both their attitudes toward customers and their ethical practices must have contained some truth. English visitors, especially—because they were accustomed to "the obsequious servility of many London shopkeepers" —were amazed and shocked at the salesmen's behavior. Moreover, in 1817, even the shopkeepers were said to have an air of "cold indifference" when a customer entered the store: never even bothering to remove their hats, they continued to "sit or lie along the counters, smoking segars, and spitting in every direction, to a degree offensive to any man of decent feelings." Some years later a visitor from Scotland thought American storekeepers "not very remarkable for politeness to their customers. They seem to think that they are rather conferring a favour upon the purchaser than otherwise."[54] Even Francis Wyse, one of the few Englishmen who praised the appearance of American stores, was in agreement about the lack of salesmanship. Particularly annoyed at the absence of "courtesy to strangers, sometimes bordering on downright rudeness," he said that the salesmen ignored and despised "the varied little attentions, so general and well understood by shopkeepers in England." An Englishwoman in 1854 pictured the Broadway clerk as "seated by the morning paper—probably balancing himself on one leg of his chair, with a spitoon by his side," completely indifferent "whether you purchase or no."[55] Even American observers complained. One said that most salesrooms were sloppy and had "groups of lazy clerks . . . *leaning* or *sitting* upon the most convenient piles of goods. This latter habit," complained the editor of the *Dry Goods Reporter*, "is never allowed in any country except this. Being able to call all the customers by their right name," he said, does "not constitute the trade of a salesman any more than the cultivation of a mustache." Rather, he added, "long years of *laborious practice* under *good instruction* will alone accomplish it, and it were well if this were more generally understood."[56]

One of the prime functions of the salesmen was to negotiate prices. This practice, especially true prior to 1835, when prices were largely determined by bargaining, was also true in later years, when prices, although stated, were frequently lowered after negotiations. One customer claimed in 1853 that he had bought a coat on Broadway for $20, although the garment had been listed by the dealer for $30. Buyers were warned to be well acquainted with the value of each article they purchased, in order to avoid paying a "penalty proportional to . . . ignorance." They were also cautioned to be on the lookout for the sharp Chatham Street traders, who were great artists "especially in coats. Step into the nearest clothing store in Chatham-Street," wrote one observer in 1849, "and slip on a coat—*any* coat—and we'll wager our wedding-suit that it is a 'splendid fit.' There is no such thing as an ill-fitting coat in Chatham-Street. Every coat there fits everybody."

The customers, however, were not the only ones to be pitied. The life of the clothing salesman was far from an easy one. His working day, which was long, lasted between twelve and sixteen hours. Moreover, at the Broadway clothing store, the cutters waited on customers between nine in the morning and nine at night. The clerks and salesmen who did not perform tailoring duties probably earned between $300 and $500 a year. For the desk jobs the clothiers preferred young men, between the ages of fourteen and eighteen, who lived at home and "who would be satisfied with a small salary." There was little need for clerks or salesmen who did not possess a knowledge of tailoring, because they, as well as the cutters, were expected to be able to fill all positions.

There was probably an oversupply of young men willing to perform selling and bookkeeping duties in retail clothing stores from the 1830's on, because such work was a proper way to get a start in the world, and few men looked upon it as anything more than temporary. Most of the young people dreamed of going into business on their own. The crisis of 1857 and the depression that followed it, however, took a heavy toll among the young men and "The Clerk's Aid Society for New York," which was formed in the spring of that year, was one attempt to help them.

VIII

THE CHALLENGE OF CHANGE

In organization and methods of production the custom tailor shop of the opening years of the nineteenth century differed little from the shop of the first years of the eighteenth century. At the top of the firm's small but hierarchical structure was the master tailor, whose reputation as a craftsman spelled the success or failure of the enterprise. With the assistance of one or more journeymen tailors and apprentices he produced merchandise for his local trade. During rush seasons he also enlisted the aid of his wife, daughters, and a few sewing women. Although the system was traditional, it was not rigid. Apprentices, who were generally hired for "terms of three, seven, or ten years," sometimes became journeymen in much shorter periods of time. As was said in 1817, "*competency*, not legal servitude, [was] the standard for employment."[1]

The shops were not mechanized and only a few inexpensive tools were needed. Skill, not machinery, was the prerequisite to success for a custom tailor shop. All that was required for cutting was a pair of shears, a tape measure, a square, and a straight ruler. In addition, a pantaloon measuring instrument, which was invented by William H. Stinemets in 1834 and which consisted simply of a tape measure attached to a square ruler,[4] was sometimes among the tools of the custom tailors. A cutting table, which seldom was larger than eleven and one-half feet by six feet, was found in the better furnished shops. "In order to have a full set of tailors instruments," wrote one authority in 1849, "you only need the square and scales, tape, shears, chalk, and curve rule." The "scales" was a pantaloon measuring instrument similar to, but more elaborate than, the one invented by Stinemets.[3] In 1854 it sold for $3. The same year squares cost between $1 and $2 and a curved ruler cost 50 cents.

The tailor, of course, had to be skilled in handling the tools. Cutting, which in the early nineteenth century included designing and fitting, was generally entrusted to the master tailor, who usually proclaimed his skill in the art. John Ditchett declared in 1808 that he had skillfully cut 10,000 garments in three years. The same year John Inglesby said that "for the future, it [was] his design to cut out the whole of his work himself." William Winterton, a custom tailor at 23 Broad Street, made a similar declaration that year, and in 1833 Jonathan M'Dona assured his patrons that "the cutting and fitting department will be exclusively confined" to himself.

With the expansion of the custom tailoring shops after the late 1830's, the cutting department was placed under the supervision of skilled assistants and the master tailor assumed the position of general overseer. Nevertheless, the cutting department remained the cornerstone of the business, and the custom tailors frequently made a point of announcing under whose charge the cutting took place. In 1842 Charles Cox said that "Mr. Babcock, long known as one of the most fashionable cutters, continues in the establishment." The following year Edward Fox, proprietor of a Broadway tailor shop, directed "attention to his superior style of cutting" and to the fact that he "employed one of the best cutters in the country," who was able to "fit the most difficult form."

The fields of designing, fitting, and cutting were in an experimental state during the forty years that preceded the Civil War. The numerous technological treatises that emerged in that period reveal that the tailors raised penetrating questions about the relationship and application of anthropometry—the science of measuring the human body and its parts—to the tailoring craft.

Shortly after the turn of the nineteenth century the tailors began to insist that their craft be based on "scientific principles," and it was not long before a host of so-called scientific principles of tailoring—quite a few of which were written by the New York tailors—were pouring off the presses. A book list compiled in 1849 included such titles as Allen Ward's *Protractor System and System of Parts,* A. C. Houston's *Delineator,* I. N. Young's *The Square and Plumb Rule* and *Madison Rule,* T. Oliver's *Square and Protractor System* and *Rule of Thirds,* Walker's *System of Measurement,* D. William's *The Tailors Measurer,* Scott's and Wilson's *Twenty Rules,* Taylor's *Double Square or Surveying System,* and W. R. Acton's *Tailors Transfer.*[4] The list was compiled by Harvey L. Eades, a student of tailoring and the author of *Tailors Division System,* which he wrote in 1849 both to prove that all the scientific systems developed previously were not quite scientific enough and to introduce some of his own ideas.

The majority of these tailoring treatises attempted to develop a table of proportions so that a person drafting a garment could, for example, by measuring the width of a customer's chest or the breadth of his shoulder, determine the lengths and widths of all other parts of the garment. Since human proportions differ so greatly, however, it was impossible to work out accurate tables on the basis of rigid scientific formulae. Nevertheless, numerous conflicting philosophies poured off the presses. E. Chesterman, who admitted in 1830 that he was aware of "the multiplicity of rules that have been introduced," insisted that "all . . . have been founded on one principle, and that an erroneous one," and claimed that according to his plan garments could be "marked out with much greater ease and expedition than by any other rule that has been published."[5] In 1837 Scott and Perkins introduced their study on tailoring to "facilitate the art of cutting garments beyond any other that has been presented to the trade." They believed that a table of proportions based on a chest measure was utterly inadequate. If you "make all men of one shape," they declared, "a system from the breast measure may be prepared to fit all men alike." But, since you do not shape them alike, they said, "drafting from the shoulder-measure" would be far more accurate, because the size of the shoulders does not differ in its proportion from the rest of the body so radically as does the size of the chest.[6]

Throughout the 1840's and 1850's system followed system, and each claimed to have the true scientific principles of drafting and cutting garments. A number of the authors emphasized that they were practicing tailors and that their conclusions were based on many years of experience. In 1840 T. Oliver advertised his "improved and unrivaled system of cutting." The following year New York tailors were confronted with "Boughton's Square Rule for Cutting Garments," which was described as "a newly discovered square principle, entirely different from all other systems of cutting, and drafted by a different measure, and the only measure that is not liable to vary from a proportion with the shoulders." David K. Boughton, the author, believed that he had given the trade "a fixed principle, that neither fashion nor prejudice will destroy." Another tailor, William H. Stinemets, gave up his fashionable tailoring shop at 5 Nassau Street in 1841 and devoted the following two years to writing *A Complete and Permanent System of Cutting All Kinds of Garments to Fit the Human Form on a New and Scientfic Principle.* The book must have proved popular in 1843, because a second edition appeared in 1844.[7] In the preface to the first edition Stinemets declared that the difficulty with all previous systems of drafting was that "all more or less, have been adapted to one particular size of coat, or only calculated for one kind of garment." His system, he said, "as laid down in this work, will produce with equal facility, not only every style of garment now in vogue, but will be equally applicable to whatever changes may take place." Stinemets, of course, was not the only tailor who insisted that his principle of cutting was unique. In 1855 Alex D. Reeves, a "tailor and teacher of the art of cutting by actual measurement," challenged all New York tailors to meet him "at the fair of the Mechanics' Institute to be held at the Crystal Palace on the 3d of October, 1855, for the purpose of placing his system of cutting in a fair trial of competition with those who may feel inclined to risk their reputation on the result."

Such challenges were characteristic of the general spirit of inquiry in the early nineteenth century in America. They were also a manifestation of the desire on the part of the tailors to systematize production techniques in order to be able to meet an expanding local demand. If a garment could be accurately drafted and cut according to the measurement of a customer's shoulder or chest, the merchants thought, endless time could be saved.

The increased local demand was met also by the complete reorganization of the custom tailor shop. Cutting rooms were enlarged to cutting departments, in which a number of craftsmen—each a specialist in trousers, waistcoats, or coats—worked side by side. In 1838 one dealer praised his excellent "vest makers." In 1851 A. and G. A. Arnoux, custom tailors, claimed to have "three skilful artists employed . . . one to cut coats, one to cut pants, and one to cut waistcoats." One young man seeking employment in 1854 advertised himself as a "cutter for pants." The following year one fellow called himself an experienced "pantaloon and vest cutter" and another offered to "cut coats exclusively."

In the larger shops a fourth man was employed in the cutting department to sponge (prepare) the cloth for cutting. The foreman, who might have been the master tailor, supervised operations, measured the customers, was present at the fittings, and sometimes helped to design the garments.

Under pressure to meet competition and to keep labor costs low, the merchants made greater use of seamstresses. These women, who were employed at their own homes, generally sewed vests and pantaloons, which were easier than coats. As early as 1817 an observer remarked that vests and pantaloons were made mostly "by women, at from 25 to 50 per cent. cheaper than if men were employed." This system of production, however, attached a stigma to the workmanship of many of the custom tailors. In 1841 the *New York Herald* wrote, "Is there a tailor in New York who can make a good fitting pair of pantaloons? We doubt it. And the reason is that they give them out to girls to sew up, who think more of their beaux than their pants. In London and Paris, pantaloons are well made—but in New York, they are all slops—slops—slops."

By the end of the 1850's the cheapest grade of custom clothes differed little from the best grade of ready-made garments. Frequently, after a custom garment was cut, the master tailor completely divorced himself from direct supervision of the remaining operations: as a result, those tasks fell under the jurisdiction of the middlemen or contractors, who assumed the responsibility for manufacturing and who employed less skilled labor than did the tailors. Even the increased use of the sewing machine in the 1850's had little impact on the production of finer products for the order trade, although the contractors, in an attempt to rush out orders of cheaper grades, made extensive use of sewing girls who were skilled in the operation of the new instrument.

The Role of Immigrant Labor in the Production of Ready-Made Clothing. Unlike the producer for the order trade, the wholesale manufacturer of ready-made apparel was faced at the very outset with the task of employing and organizing a tremendous labor force of highly skilled and semiskilled male and female workers. As early as 1836 leading wholesalers employed between 300 and 500 workers each.[8] The majority of the employees were tailors and tailoresses who sewed, since only a handful of cutters was needed. The proportion of tailors and tailoresses to cutters is evident in an advertisement of Hobby, Husted and Co., which in 1836 sought 300 tailors, 500 tailoresses, and six cutters "accustomed to southern work."[9] That year another firm asked for "800 good plain sewers." Further, it was estimated that year that 10,000 women in the city "depended on the needle for a support." This figure probably included dressmakers and millinery workers; still, a good many of the women were engaged solely as tailoresses for the ready-to-wear firms.

Compared to those of the 1850's, however, those figures were small. One house, Hanford and Brother, employed more than 2,000 people in 1855. Three years later the New York Chamber of Commerce reported that one clothing house "gives employment to more hands at this moment than were employed by all the houses in the wholesale clothing trade thirty years ago."[10] The census of 1860 said that "so extensive have some of the wholesale clothing houses become" in New York City "that several thousand persons have been employed by a single establishment." That report counted 21,568 people employed in the New York clothing trade, including employees of custom tailor shops, but not including those engaged in manufacturing shirts, collars, and men's furnishings.

Obviously, "human machinery" was an indispensible factor in the production of clothing. And, since New York City was a prime receiver of immigrants from Western Europe, it was in a masterful position to supply that "machinery."

Visitors from abroad constantly reminded their countrymen back home of the grand opportunities awaiting tailors in the Empire City. Tailors in America, they said, received wages that were one-third higher than they were in England. "The tailors are the best remunerated mechanics in America," wrote Andrew Bell in 1836. "A good cutter will always receive steady employment and good wages" here, advised Francis Wyse nine years later. Wyse added that tailors were generally "paid well." Moreover, the New York clothing manufacturers themselves tried to attract European labor.[11]

Of the 5,457,914 alien passengers who arrived in the United States between 1820 and 1860, 3,742,532 entered at New York harbor, and a good many of them went right into the city's clothing industry. The industry throve upon the immigrants for entrepreneurs as well as laborers. Between 1820 and 1860, 3,634 tailors and 5,246 seamstresses and milliners entered the United States, and many of them set up businesses in New York. Of the 403 clothiers in the city in 1855, 304 were born abroad. Of these, 159 were from Germany, 81 from Ireland, 23 from England, and the rest from nine other countries. Of the 12,609 tailors in the city in 1855, 12,109 were foreign-born; of these, 6,709 were from Germany, 4,171 from Ireland, 501 from England, and the rest from about 20 other countries.[12]

German and Irish immigrants constitued the principal source of labor for the clothing manufacturers. Hanford and Brother claimed that its "male employees are principally German and Irish—few Americans being employed in it, except as cutters."[13] Although most of the original sewing women employed were Americans, they began to be displaced during the heavy immigration of the 1840's; and within twenty years immigrant women, most of whom were Irish, had assumed a dominant role in the cheaper grade sewing operations.

One example of an immigrant who rose to own and manage his own clothing firm was P. L. Rogers, who arrived in New York from Ireland at the age of eighteen and moved rapidly from a tailor's apprentice to a small shopkeeper and finally to the leadership of one of the largest clothing houses in 1850—a six-story establishment at the corner of Fulton and Nassau streets that employed more than 1,000 people.

Organization of the Inside Shop in the Production of Ready-Made Clothing. Although the majority of the sewers employed by wholesale manufacturers worked in their own homes—the outside shop—the key operations were performed under the immediate supervision of the employer and his foremen in the inside shop. In the shop the cloth was received, examined, sponged, cut, and bundled before either being given out or sewed on the premises. In many respects the organization of production operations was similar to that in the large order houses: the differences were quantitative rather than qualitative. The wholesale shops' investment in machinery and tools was of minimum importance. An investigation of 126 tailor shops in the city in 1855 showed that only a little more than $50,000 was invested in tools and machinery.[14]

Some of the extended wholesale operations, however, necessitated a form of regulated operation and organization that went far beyond that found in even the largest custom tailor houses. In 1857 "one feature of the ready-made clothing manufacture, peculiarly deserving of commendation, is the thorough system with which the operations are conducted. In the large establishments everything is carried on with the regularity of clock-work." The same observer described the routine of the larger houses as follows:

"As soon as a piece of cloth has been received into the store, it is carefully examined, and the blemished portions, if any, withdrawn. After this examination, each piece is taken to the superintendent with a memorandum of the quantity it contains, its cost, of whom purchased, etc., all of which is entered in a book; also, the number and description of garments to be made; how trimmed; name of cutter, price of making, etc. It is then passed to the cutter, who receives directions as to the kind, style, and size of the article to be made; and after being cut, the pieces are handed over to the trimmer, who supplies buttons, thread, lining, etc. The goods are then received by one of the foremen, who gives them out to be sewed and finished; and on their return they are examined by him, and forwarded to the sales department."[15]

This procedure was generally followed by such firms as C. T. Longstreet and Co., Brooks Brothers, Lewis and Hanford, D. J. Devlin, and Alfred Munroe and Co. The labor force was never large in the inside shop. Brooks employed 78 people on the premises and more than 1,500 outside. Lewis and Hanford in 1849 employed 72 people inside and 3,600 outside.[16]

The inside shop was divided into departments, and the cutting department, as in the custom tailor shop, was the most important. Lewis and Hanford had "two large rooms for cutting and trimming." At the plant of D. J. Devlin an entire floor "containing several well lighted rooms" was delegated "to the cutting department." And the cutting department, in turn, was sectioned into workshops—one "for coats; a second for pants; a third for vests; and a fourth for trimmings."

Foremen, who were sometimes business partners, supervised the cutting operations. These superintendents were generally top-notch designers and cutters and they received the highest salaries in the trade.[17] These facts were also true of the wholesale cutters, who were the most respected craftsmen in their profession. In the large clothing house of Scofield, Phelps and Co., William Scofield, the son of the founder, functioned as a cutter.[18] From the mid-1830's on, the cutters employed by the wholesalers were distinguished from the cutters employed by the order trade, and advertisements for wholesale cutters usually required a familiarity with "southern work," the ability to work quickly, and some knowledge of the mass production techniques of larger houses.

No cutting machine was in use in the men's garment industry prior to the 1870's. Although a machine "capable of cutting out fifteen suits at once" had been invented in France during the Crimean War by "Dussantey, the Emperor's tailor," and had been put to use in a large Parisian clothing factory soon after, it had made little impact on the New York industry, which relied on heavy shears. One writer noted in 1856 that in the large clothing houses "cutters of skill . . . never cease to click their shears."[19]

The cutters in the large houses paid less attention to size and fit than did the cutters in the order trade, in which considerable attention was paid to fitting each customer. The wholesale houses cut garments to fit a range of individuals. Because standard sizes were not available before 1866, each dealer set up sizes based on his own experience. As a result, advertisements that stated that "gentlemen can be as well fitted from the shelves as if their measure were taken" must be read today with considerable doubt. Further, sizes were seldom described with accuracy. In 1846 one firm described its overcoats as "varying in size from the man of three hundred to the man of three years." Six years later another claimed that its ready-made stock was "suited for tall men and short men, stout men and thin men, old men and young men, fast boys and slow boys." The wholesale houses that had a custom trade department, too, determined the sizes for the wholesale garments by the sizes made in the custom department. It was not until after the Civil War that sufficient data was available to set up standardized tables of proportions, and these were based largely on the measurements of the millions of conscripts. The initial spade work in this area was done by Brevet Brigadier General G. H. Crosman who commanded the Philadelphia Quartermaster Depot during the Civil War. In 1865 he undertook a study "intended to fix the forms, sizes . . . of the various articles of equipment which are supplied by the Quartermaster's department."[20]

By 1850 the organizational setup of the houses also included an "examining and folding department," in which goods were received and examined before being folded and stored. At times the storage department reached immense proportions. The Devlin firm devoted its entire basement to storing cloth. By 1860 the "stock Keeper" of a clothing warehouse was considered a professional. That year one clothing house sought "a young man as stock keeper" and said that "only such as have had experience in the business, and knows how to fold and assort goods need apply."[21] Finally, fabrics were sponged before they were folded and stored, so that the shrinkage would set in before the goods were cut. The sponging operation was performed either by the stock man or his sponger.[22]

Although prior to 1850 most sewing operations were performed outside the clothing plant at the homes of the contractors or the tailors and tailoresses, the popularization of the sewing machine in that decade saw a huge section of the warehouse cut off to accommodate as many as "five or six hundred operatives." Thus, by 1860 there was a more balanced proportion between the inside and outside workers. That year, one firm employed "five hundred hands in the shop, and eight hundred outside." The sewing machine, which was used more and more, but which was relatively expensive and beyond the means of many tailors and sewing girls, had necessitated the creation of vast indoor sewing accommodations. Moreover, by the end of 1850 merchants were even advertising for operators who would sew in the inside shop.

Women generally predominated in the inside shop in the sewing of vests and trousers. "An American tailor thinks it beneath his dignity to make anything but coats," wrote a traveler in 1836, adding that "waistcoats, trousers . . . are all made by females." Some years later a boys' clothing manufacturer remarked that "women excell as vest makers—a branch almost exclusively confined to them."[23] Numerous men did, however, work in the manufacturing of trousers and vests. In fact, in the summer of 1850 the New York "pantaloon makers," all of the men employed in the production of "southern pantaloons," demanded higher compensation for their work. Nevertheless, the sewing of top coats and overcoats—items that required more skill and strength in handling—and the pressing of garments with gas- or coal-heated irons were the areas in which the men were most in demand.

Children were few in the clothing warehouses. The only work available for them was a little sewing, pulling out bastings, sewing on buttons, and running errands. In 1860 one firm claimed that its "basters are only small girls." Five years earlier a clothing house had advertised for "a little girl to go errands and make herself useful."[24] Such notices, however, were rare.

Organization of the Inside Shop in the Production of Shirts, Collars, and Cuffs. In the production of shirts, collars, and cuffs there was a greater reliance upon the use of both machinery and female labor than there was in the manufacture of coats, vests, and trousers.

The wholesale production of shirts, which began about 1840, lost little time in becoming mechanized and systematized, and by 1850 most of the shirt factories' production operations were mechanized. The shirt manufactory of Winchester and Davis, which maintained a New York office at 22 Warren Street and a factory in New Haven, relied as little as possible on human hands. Cartons of cotton and linen cloth entered the basement from the srteet "by an inclined plane railway."[25] The large demand for water, which was especially great in the laundry department, was taken care of in the basement by a "force pump, worked by a steam engine, forcing water from a well to a large tank on the top of the buildings, whence it is distributed all over them."

Mechanization prevailed in the cutting room, too, where "upon long tables the cloth is spread out, lying thickness upon thickness . . . to the number of forty-eight, and upon them are placed iron patterns of all sizes. The knife does the rest, no scissors being employed." After that, all the waste was collected, because Winchester and Davis were aware that "the unavoidable clippings from this room are worth $1,000 per year for paper rags."

The knife, rather than the shears, was used by the shirt and collar producers two decades before it was used by the manufacturers of coats, vests, and pants. Since special skill was required in the use of the knife, an advertisement for a cutter of shirts and collars in 1856 declared that "none need apply but those accustomed to cut with a knife."[26]

As in other branches of the industry, much of the sewing was originally given out to tailoresses who worked at home. With the introduction of the sewing machine into the shirt, collar, and cuff industry early in 1850's, however, a good portion of the work was moved to the inside shop.

Sewing was classified into four groups. The first, as one contemporary reported, "is called plain sewing and consists simply in making the bodies; the second is called stitching and requires considerable neatness—the breasts, wrists, and collars, are stitched; the third is the finishing process, in which there is a great deal of gathering to be done, besides the stitching of the button holes and the sewing on of the buttons; the fourth is embroidering. In some stores they give the entire shirt to one person to make, while in others they distribute them in parts and classify their sewers into body makers, stitchers, finishers, and embroiderers."[27]

By the mid-1850's advertisements in the New York newspapers specifically required experienced plain sewers, finishers, fitters, body-makers, buttonhole-makers, and shirt-collar-makers. The tendency was toward defining and simplifying each sewing operation. One seamstress, who was employed at a sewing machine in a shirt factory prior to the Civil War, recalled that her "duties were defined and simple, and there was no unreasonable hurry, and no night work."[28]

Whether the sewing was done inside or outside, at the final stage of production the clothes were washed, starched, dried, and ironed by the manufacturer. Not all producers, however, had facilities on their premises for these operations. Hanford and Brother, which produced shirts as well as outer clothing, sent large quantities to Hoboken, where the shirts were "starched and done up." Winchester and Davis erected in New Haven a building with "accommodations for fifty washers and twenty-five starchers," all of whom were women. The system for washing, starching, drying, and ironing was as follows:

"Each washer has her tub and steam-boiler beside, in which she can 'boil her clothes' in five minutes. The starching arrangements are equally admirable. There is one division with eight compartments, each holding four pails full of startch. . . . Under this detached building is a reservoir, 50 by 32 feet, twelve feet deep, for holding rain water, capable of containing 130,000 gallons. . . . The shirts are now ready for the drying room, up to which they are hoisted. This is at the top of the buildings, and is 120 by 40 feet in extent. Here lines are ranged, upon which 150 dozen shirts can be hung at once. It is calculated that 225 dozen can be dried per day . . . after the shirts . . . go to the ironing rooms. Of these there are two, each one 120 by 40 feet in extent. In each are three heaters, capable of accommodating seventy-five ironers. These heaters are of extremely ingenious description, being surrounded by sheet iron cases that cause them to do double duty, in heating the irons, and passing the heat up to the drying room. . . .

The cost of supplying these heaters per day, with coal, is about seventy-five cents for each one. . . . Each of these rooms is furnished with facilities for heating water, by boilers upon the heaters. When the goods are thus completed, they are passed to be examined and repaired if necessary, before being packed in papers for market."[29]

Although a number of shirt manufacturers did produce collars and cuffs, too, the manufacture of those items was frequently a specialty of factories that produced no shirts. The production of men's collars had emerged as a separate branch of business in the mid-1820's, and, by the eve of the Civil War mechanized and systematized collar and cuff manufactories turned out thousands of those items every minute. Packed "in boxes of a dozen or a hundred" and sold "at two or three cents apiece," they enabled a purchaser to "appear once or twice a day in all the glory of an apparently clear shirt" by merely changing his collar. One Troy, New York, collar manufactory, whose product was sold largely through New York City and Philadelphia jobbers, maintained "forty-five stitching machines in daily operation . . . producing an average of 500 dozen collars per day."

By 1850 the collar manufacturers had a special apparatus that pressed and added gloss to a shirt collar in one operation. This ingeniously devised machine had "a grooved roller, suited to the shape of the collar, and covered with flannel. The iron is bevelled to fit the groove, and is warmed by a red-hot heater placed in a cavity—this iron is secured to the short arm of the lever, which is attached to another lever or treadle, one end of which is fastened to the floor. The attendant, by pressing with her foot upon one end of the lower lever, is enabled to use great power, while she turns the wooden roller on which the collar is placed. This great pressure aids in giving the gloss."[30]

Collars were generally prepared in a continuous process from "rolls many hundred feet long." After an enameling process that took about five minutes, the entire strip was "cut by knives into the different shapes and sizes required . . . so rapidly that a man and boy could make more than ten thousand in an hour." Since many of the collars were made of paper, imitation stitches "resembling the best work of a sewing machine" were printed on them. In one factory two girls attended "these machines, and . . . produced nearly a hundred collars per minute, or about sixty thousand daily." The final step—the punching of buttonholes—was performed "with even greater rapidity." After that the collars "were counted . . . put in boxes, and were ready for market."

Cuffs, which by the mid-1840's were also produced on a wholesale basis,[31] were probably manufactured by similar processes.

The Outside Shop. Although the system of employing seamstresses to work in their homes was somewhat altered after the popularization of the sewing machine—at which time a greater amount of sewing was done in the factories—it nevertheless remained in effect to a large extent until many years after the Civil War.

The outside shop was almost completely dominated by female labor. This was due not only to the almost natural proficiency of women with a needle but also to the fact that in the early years of the nineteenth century few opportunities in other than sewing and domestic work were open to women. One traveler in New York City in 1829 said that "women are not allowed to work out of doors, and work within doors must be found for them."[32]

No sooner was the wholesale manufacture of men's clothing launched into full swing than the demand for needlewomen became tremendous. Throughout the first half of the century, with the exception of the slack years of 1837 to 1842, newspaper advertisements revealed that employers were seeking tailoresses and seamstresses by the hundreds. Moreover, the dependence upon the domestic facilities of the sewing girls was evident in the occasional advertisements in which manufacturers voiced a preference for tailoresses with large families. Prior to 1845 the majority of the women engaged in domestic sewing were of American birth. After that date a great number of immigrant women, most of them Irish and German, joined the profession, and by 1860 it was estimated that only 20 per cent of the sewing women employed by one large wholesaler were American-born.[33]

Two ways were open for seamstresses to receive work—directly from the wholesale house or indirectly through a contractor who acted as a middleman between the wholesaler and the sewing women.

A number of the large New York manufacturers issued work directly to the women through a foreman, or "piecemaster," whose primary task was to give out and receive the work. The jobs to be sewed were handed out in bundles containing the cut pieces, buttons, and linings. After it was sewed and finished, the work was returned to the warehouse and examined by the foreman. If he was satisfied, he paid the tailoresses. The piecemaster was an important link between the inside and outside shops, and he drew one of the highest salaries in the clothing trade: it ranged as high as "$150 dollars per week" in the mid-1850's.[34] In some houses the piecemasters were also skilled cutters, and they supervised the cutting operations inside, as well as the distribution of work outside. In the larger houses, however, their task remained confined to distribution and receipt. One advertisement in

1847 made no mention of cutting skill when it called for "a man to take charge of the work hands (give out and receive work) in a large clothing house. He must be well acquainted with this branch and of active and steady business habits. A good salary will be paid to one who can fill this situation."[35]

Sewing women applying for work were generally expected to submit samples of their needlework. "Wanted," said one advertisement in 1836, "a few good hands, to make . . . coats . . . apply, with sample of work." A call for "first class fine vest makers" some years later said that the applicants "must bring a sample of their own make." Occasionally a "good reference" was used as a substitute for a sample; but more often both were required. One wholesaler declared that "the character of work done by applicants is judged of by turning to the book of their former employer, and seeing what prices were paid." After the introduction of the sewing machine, the girls were sometimes asked to perform a task on the machine as a test.

When they received work, the sewing women were told to return the completed job by a specified time. To insure the return of the work, the employers collected a deposit as security against damage to, or loss of, the goods. The deposit ranged from about $1 for $8 worth of merchandise to the full value of the materials. In addition, each seamstress was expected "to procure herself a book in which the quantity and value of the goods" and the security left were entered. At times the hardships entailed in raising the security were enormous, and many complaints were voiced. On some occasions the deposit was not returned on the plea that the job had been done unsatisfactorily. Sometimes "the condemned garment [was even] ripped asunder and returned to the women to be resewed, the money being witheld until the complete order is approved." By 1861 some firms had ceased the demand for a deposit, considering "a recommendation from the last employer" and a sample task sufficient. That year one foreman saw little need for collecting security. He declared that he had "never lost anything by girls not returning goods. If they should keep them, they would soon be known at the different establishments, and have no place to go for work."[36]

The sewing women were drawn not only from the urban area in which they were situated but also from the surrounding country farms and hamlets. Hobby, Husted and Co. announced in 1836 that "persons living at a distance may receive large quantities of clothing to be made up in the country." Hanford and Brother gave much of its cheaper grade sewing to country girls, as did other firms. In fact, New

York clothing was sewed throughout New York, New Jersey, and Connecticut.

In many cases work was distributed to the country workers through a contractor, who assumed charge of the sewing operations for a stipulated fee. One contractor advertised in 1834 that he was seeking "to obtain employment for a number of industrious young ladies in a country village" and that he "would be willing to make a contract with the proprietor of a clothing warehouse . . . who has plenty of work to do, and wants it done well." The contractor assumed responsibility for both the conveyance of the clothing to the country homes and the return of the completed jobs to the manufacturers.

By the 1840's the system of subcontracting had removed some sewers three steps from the original manufacturer. This subcontracting occurred when one contractor passed the goods on to another who, in turn, became responsible for their manufacture. Not too popular in New York City prior to the Civil War, contracting and subcontracting were usually employed only in the manufacture of the lowest grade of garments. After the invention of the sewing machine the contractors depended more upon the urban tailoresses, who were able to work in shops that had such machines or who owned their own machines.

If the stories handed down to us about the outside shops are only half true, the conditions in them, even at their best, were miserable. Since work was paid by the piece and deadlines had to be met, hours were usually long. "I have often sat a whole day and far into the night, in making a single shirt," recalled one seamstress.[37] With living rooms and kitchens converted into workshops, the remaining conveniences of homes were few. The fact that the children and the aged had to help in the sewing task made the picture even sadder. In addition, the poor lighting and lack of ventilation in the tenements, where most of the work was done, made the atmosphere more depressing.

Further, in order to conserve rent, some girls—in one case, six—rented a room in which they sewed and slept on the floor "on straw beds." In another case three girls rented a room in which they worked "day and night": they divided the work so that "two baste and finish off, and one operates." One observer wrote that "some of the poor tailors in New York rent a room, occupy a spot themselves, and rent out the rest of the room to others . . . charging fifty cents for seat room for a man and a girl to assist him; thirty-seven cents for a man alone."[38]

Child labor was undoubtedly at its worst in the outside shops. Although no statistics are available, numerous children must have worked long hours beside their elders. Some tailoresses even hired "young girls" to assist them. A New York newspaper reported in 1853 that "these young girls, since they are classified as 'learners' may not get any pay—or very little or just a place to sleep and a meal."[39]

The only bright spot that could be detected in the outside shops was the fact that the work was not usually hurried or rigidly supervised and, as a result, time could be taken out for frequent lunches and chats.

The Sewing Machine. Although the sewing machine's full impact was not felt by the clothing industry in the half century before 1861, its invention should be considered the outstanding technological innovation of that period.

Numerous minds and hands tinkered with the idea of developing a sewing machine from 1755 on. However, the basic invention and improvements can be attributed to only a handful of individuals. The first device that can be classed as a sewing machine was really no more than an embroidering machine conceived by an Englishman, Charles F. Weisenthal, in 1755. His idea probably did little more than kindle the imagination of other inventors. Thirty-five years later another Englishman, Thomas Saint, received a patent for a machine that sewed leather with a needle and thread. Although the machine was a revolution in sewing, no practical use was made of Saint's idea.[40] As a result, it was not until 1829 that the first sewing machine that was to undergo a practical test in a clothing factory was conceived. This apparatus was devised by Barthelemy Thimonnier, a poor French tailor and part-time inventor. The following year his machine, which made a chain stitch with a hooked needle, was patented, and in 1831, 80 of the devices were installed in a clothing factory that produced uniforms for French troops. The machines were short-lived, however, because angry tailors, who saw a threat to their ancient ways, smashed every one of them and forced their inventor to flee for his life to England. In that country he was able to improve his invention, and in 1849 he received a patent for it from the United States.

By that time, American inventors, too, had entered the sewing field. Unhampered by the conservative ways of the tailors' guilds these inventors raised the sewing machine to practical perfection and won universal acceptance for it. One of the first inventors, a New York Quaker, Walter Hunt, invented between 1832 and 1834 in his shop on Amos Street the most practical machine in existence up to that time. Although the machine had weaknesses—it could not sew curves or angles or work a continuous seam for more than a few inches, and it had an imperfect cloth feed that made it cumbersome to operate—it was far ahead of all other machines.

Elias Howe, Jr., a New England machinist, was also an important contributor to the sewing machine's development. He began devising a model in 1839; when his task was completed in 1845 he found that his greatest difficulty was convincing others of the utility of his contribution. Unsuccessful in the United States, he moved his model and his family to England in the hopes of meeting more appreciative tailors. After a few discouraging years he returned to the United States (in 1849) only to find that other inventors had entered the field and had, he felt, infringed on the patent that had been granted to him in 1846.

By 1850 the tailoring community had become conscious of the sewing machine and numerous inventive minds had gone to work on perfecting it. Although Howe's machine had been the most practical prior to 1850, there was room for considerable improvement and every change was observed closely. Ten sewing machine patents were granted prior to 1850,[41] nearly three hundred patents were granted between 1850 and 1859, and 607 were granted by 1863.

But the outstanding advances after Howe must be attributed to another New England machinist, Isaac M. Singer. Other inventors had thought of slight improvements on Howe's machine, but Singer had introduced a fundamental correction. The sewing machines that had preceded Singer's model had lacked an adequate arrangement for the application of power to drive them. Since they used a hand crank they required the operator's right hand. As a result, only the left could arrange and guide the material. Singer's innovations were a rocking treadle, upon which both feet were placed, and a balance wheel on the upper shaft that increased momentum when the machine was in motion. Since the machine was operated largely by a heel-and-toe motion on the rocking treadle, both hands were free for work.[42]

On the same day on which Singer was granted his patent—August 12, 1851—Allen B. Wilson was granted a patent for a model that he had designed independently and that contained features absent on both the Singer and Howe models. The Wilson model was lighter in weight—it was advertised as weighing six and one-half pounds to Singer's fifty-five—and it contained a rotary hook, a four-motion feed, and a circular disk bobbin. A stock company incorporated under the name of Wheeler, Wilson Manufacturing Company in 1853 lost little time in making the Wilson model the strongest competitor of the Singer machine.[43]

The development of still another type of machine—one with an improved stitch—was achieved by a oBston tailor, William O. Grover, whose patent was issued on February 11, 1851. Grover introduced a machine that sewed two pieces of cloth with two threads at once: the threads interlocked to form "the double-locked chain stitch." The Grover and Baker Sewing Machine Company was formed shortly after to manufacture and sell the machine.

The subsequent invention of James E. A. Gibbs further improved the firmness of the stitch. Gibbs introduced a sewing machine that performed a chain stitch, or lock-stitch, with a single thread. The idea was patented in June, 1857, and the Willcox and Gibbs Sewing Machine Company was formed to market it.

The sewing machine, however, was not accepted without resentment. Objections against its use were based upon economic, as well as moral and technological, reasons. Violent destruction of the machines was absent in the United States, but resentment and fear that the device would injure thousands who were dependent upon the needle for a living was not. "Suppose that a sewing machine were invented to-morrow, which should do the work of the thousands of women," asked Robert Dale Owen as early as 1830, "would it not take the bread from their mouths?"[44] Because the machines were expected to throw thousands of sewing women into poverty, they caused some employers to have doubts about their immediate adoption. The *New-York Daily Tribune* urged women in June, 1853, to train for other pursuits and warned that the widespread use of the sewing machine might force them to "sink back into a state of Oriental debasement and abject dependence."[45] The sewing machine did in fact cause a reduction of wages to hand sewers. "I was confounded," wrote a seamstress, "at the low rates to which wages fell. The price for making a shirt was reduced one half . . . Even the mean slop-shop work was so poorly paid, that no women, working full time, could earn more than a dollar a week."[46]

The question of wages, however, could not halt for long the advance of the new technique. Many of the hand sewers who wasted little time in learning how to operate the new instrument found, to their surprise, that the adjustment was not very difficult to make. The census of 1860 reported that "the recent introduction of the sewing-machine . . . has reduced the number of sewing women, and their sudden displacement in some places may have been injuriously felt without on the whole damaging their interests as a class." And that observation was correct since, after all, the one thing that the sewing machine did not alter was the character of the labor force: women still continued to dominate the field of sewing.

Objections to the machines were also based on technological arguments and the question of price. The early machines were greeted with little faith by the manufacturers of clothing and, although it was displayed at the Crystal Palace exhibition in London in 1851, the new gadget was almost completely ignored by contemporary observers. The original machines were cumbersome and difficult to operate and their speed scarcely exceeded that of human hands. In addition they were expensive—in the early 1850's they sold for between $100 and $150—and few producers cared to make the initial investment for the installation of a dozen or more machines.

A general prejudice against the sewing machines remained throughout the 1850's. Nevertheless, the machines increased in popularity throughout the United States much more quickly than they did in any other part of the world. Visiting New York City in 1854, one Englishman was amazed at "the readiness with which machinery is introduced into all branches of industry. They have machines," he observed, "for making shirts . . . machines for sewing, at which one woman can do as much as twenty with the hand."[47]

When the French government studied the question of installing sewing machines in the production of army uniforms in 1855 it invited a New York seamstress to demonstrate the instrument. Elated by the results, the French government not only showered the seamstress with gifts and "a salary of 750 francs a month" and urged her to continue her demonstrations but also thought of sending to New York for additional machines, "as well as for girls to work them." One sign of the increasing popularity of the sewing machine in 1855 was the trade that had been begun in second-hand models. That year one dealer advertised for 25 Singer and 25 Grover and Baker second-hand machines.

By the end of the 1850's the more mechanical-minded observers were so excited by the results of the sewing machine that some of them dared to speculate about the future. According to one writer in 1859, it was hoped that a new machine would be invented not only to sew two pieces of cloth together but also to manufacture an entire garment. "The problem," he wrote, "will not be difficult to solve; and he who first solves it, shall be famous amongst men."[48]

The ultimate gradual acceptance of the sewing machine by the clothing manufacturers, tailors, and seamstresses was no doubt due in part to the promotional techniques utilized by the device's manufacturers, such as Isaac M. Singer and Co. At his Broadway manufactory Singer furnished a group of lavishly decorated showrooms to which he invited visitors and prospective buyers and in which he had attractive women seated before huge mirrors operating his machines.[49] He used every possible inducement to push his product into the market. In 1853 he allowed seamstresses to purchase his machine on the installment plan. Later he permitted liberal discounts to all who wished to trade their old models of any brand for one of his new machines, and in 1856 he announced that "the Avery, Wilson, Grover & Baker, Hunt . . . and other inferior machines, are coming in rapidly to be exchanged." His newspaper advertisements cleverly stressed the names of the large clothing firms that had installed his machines, and to seamstresses and tailoresses he constantly pointed out his latest improvements—such as the noiselessness of the machines—and stressed the boost in earnings that the ownership of a machine would make possible.

The manufacturers of sewing machines were well aware that one of the strongest inducements to buying a machine would be the knowledge of how to operate one. Therefore, little time was wasted in setting up schools in the major cities so that women could learn the technique of a faultless performance. One seamstress recalled: "The school was in reality a mere show-shop, a place of exhibition established by the machine-makers, in which to display and advertise their wares more thoroughly to the public. We pupils were the unconscious mouthpieces of the manufacturers. We paid the teacher for the privilege of learning to work the machines, and the manufacturers paid her a commission for all that she disposed of. Between the two sets of contributors to her purse she must have done a profitable business. She was at no expense except for rent, as the manufacturers loaned her the machines, while we did all the work."[50]

The impact of the sewing machine on the production of clothing can be seen clearly in the last few years of the 1850's, when the manufacture of sewing machines reached enormous heights. In a twelve-month period—between the fall of 1858 and the fall of 1859—more than 37,000 sewing machines were produced in the United States. As a result, the prices for the machines decreased and in 1858 new models could be bought for as low as $50.[51]

According to a government survey in 1860 the popularity of the sewing machine was largely responsible for the "silent revolution which took place in the business structure of the clothing trade." It was "chiefly through the agency of the sewing machine," the report declared, that "many small shops have been merged into large wholesale establishments for the manufacture and sale of ready-made clothing." The survey further pointed out that although the capital investment in the clothing industry doubled between 1850 and 1860, the number of clothing establishments decreased by 11 per cent.

The sewing machine also increased the size and importance of the inside shop, because many women who had sewed at home turned to the operation of machines on the employers' premises. Moreover, lack of skill did not prove to be a great obstacle: the skilled taught the unskilled and "operatives were multiplied almost as rapidly as the machines." In addition, the sewing machine introduced a still greater division of labor into the production process. Whereas each hand sewer had previously been assigned a complete garment, each operator now sewed one or two seams and passed the unfinished garment on to another operator. In 1859 a factory in Cincinnati had divided the labor of its operators so finely that "as many as seventeen hands [were] employed upon a single pair of pants. Any of these, if even a novice in sewing, has so small a portion to execute, that she can readily acquire a due proficiency in her single department."[52]

In some cases the sewing machines, as well as the needle and thread, were supplied by the operators themselves. It is quite probable also that the cost for fuel—by 1860 sewing machines in a few factories were driven by steam power—was charged to the operator.

The sewing machine also left its mark on the outside shop, because each person who owned a machine gained an initial advantage in the transition period. Further, advertisements for workers made it clear that owners of sewing machines were preferred. As a result, those who did not own a machine often rented one from the contractor who furnished their work. The period in which hand-sewing changed to machine-sewing must have been disturbing and discouraging to many of the seamstresses of the old school. "Thousands of sewing-girls, all over the country," wrote a seamstress, "were . . . astonished and disheartened, when they came to be assured of the success of these machines." The majority, however, lost little time in dropping their needles and rapidly mastering the new technique. One seamstress wrote that she had suddenly realized that she "had overlooked the important fact that all sewing for the public was still to be done by women, even though machines had been invented on which to do it; in our first depression, we had innocently supposed that in future it was to be done by men. It was obvious, then, that our only course was to get machines—one for my mother, and one for myself. I knew that I should learn quickly."[53]

The sewing machine, however, did not create a great change in the dismal productive setup of the outside shop. The only possibility is that the constant noise of the machine shortened the working hours, so that the sleep of family and neighbors wouild not be disturbed.

But it was not long before hand-sewing became a dying art. By 1861 people complained that it was "not easy to get good hand tailoresses, for most are employed by machines."

Because the sewing machine enabled one person to do the work of ten or twenty, it seemed to mean that the needs of the clothing trade would be answered by a greatly diminished labor force. However, fewer tailors and tailoresses were not employed in 1860 than in 1850; rather, the growing demand for ready-made clothing spurred production to such heights that the need for labor far outstripped any saving in labor offered by the machine. This situation was reported with some surprise in the first annual report of the New York State Chamber of Commerce in 1859. Referring to the sewing machine, it said that it was "strange . . . that whilst it [the machine] greatly increases the capacity to produce, [it] does not diminish the demand for manual labor; on the contrary, there are more hands employed now than ever before. The very increase in the production of the article induces a corresponding increase in the consumption. It would seem that 'appetite grows by what it feeds upon.'"

The wages of the tailors and tailoresses were not ultimately affected very greatly, if at all, by the sewing machine. Moreover, any saving in wages that did occur was not passed on to the operator and was actually no saving for the manufacturer, who had to buy, install, and maintain the new machines. Even the tailoresses who bought their own machines experienced no real gain in earnings, because any increases were offset by the expense of the purchase. On the other hand, however, the seamstresses who refused to turn to the machine found themselves economically strangled, because the demand for hand labor had almost disappeared.

Thus, the invention and popularization of the sewing machine was the outstanding technological achievement of the clothing industry prior to the Civil War. It is difficult to imagine how the New York clothing industry would have met the tremendous demand that arose in the 1850's without the machine. Moreover, the relatively quick acceptance of the machine speaks well of the pliability of both the clothing manufacturers and tailors and tailoresses, most of whom were quick to see the device's benefits.

IX

LABOR'S CAUSE

In considering the wages paid to New York clothing workers during the first sixty years of the nineteenth century, it must be remembered that adequate statistical information is unobtainable and that contemporary statements of wages are largely those of biased observers who championed the cause of either the garment workers or the employers. In addition, work was seasonal in character and a weekly statement of wages sheds little light on yearly earnings. In fact, for many rural tailoresses the work was a part-time pursuit, and yearly earnings from sewing were only a part of the total yearly income. Further, little information is available about the working day in the various clothing houses, which probably ranged between ten and fourteen hours. In the outside shop there was even less uniformity, because the length of the working day varied according to the extent of each job and the number of members in each household.

Information concerning the wages earned in the inside shop is almost completely lacking for the years prior to 1849. And what information there is must be viewed in the light of the various expenses that the employees were often expected to assume, such as thread, needles, fuel for heating the irons, and sewing machines.

Despite these obstacles, however, some statements can be made about wages. The gap between the wages paid to tailors and those paid to tailoresses was striking. The tailors, who were considered the more skilled members of the profession and who received the more difficult tasks, were paid throughout most of the period by the "piece" or "job." What constituted a job in 1800, however, did not constitute one by 1850, because more and more "extras" were continuously introduced. Thus, by 1850 almost every part of a coat, vest, or pair of trousers had become an "extra" and was paid for separately.

"The New York Journeymen Tailors' Bill of Prices for Southern Trade" in 1850 offers an idea of the payments for various jobs performed on a "cloth and cashmere dress or frock coat." The minimum work brought a payment of $2.50. Such "extras" as the following called for additional compensation:

Padded lapelles	12½c
Padded collars, 5 rows in stand, 9 in fall	18½c
Side edges, half or full length	18½c
Stitching front edges, one back and upper side cuffs	37½c
Side lining creased in half-inch blocks	12½c
Silk or alpaca shoulders, creased in half-inch squares	25c
Tob back lining, plain, silk or alpaca neck-pad, not exceeding six rows	6¼c
V stitched in skirt lining of frock or dress coats, four rows in each side, six inches long by four wide	25c
Flower stitched in side-lining	25c[1]

The "Pantaloon Makers," who also published a "Bill of Prices" in 1850, revealed that the minimum work on a pair of "pants of black or blue cashmere, doeskin, etc." brought seventy-five cents, and that a list of ten "extras" included such tasks as sewing "canvas in bottom" and "binding tape" or "cords down the side." Thus, by the end of the 1850's the list of "extras" had become extensive.[2] Further, through these extra payments the tailors were able by 1850 to earn a daily minimum wage of $1.

Since by August 19, 1850, sixty-nine clothing firms—included Devlin and Co., Weyman and Co., Degroot and Co., Stilwell and Montross, Rogers and Co., and Brooks Brothers—were paying the prices presented above,[3] one might assume that by that date most tailors were earning about $1 a day. Many, however, were earning more. One traveler observed in 1850 that "in regard to the rate of wages it may be stated generally that . . . tailors earn about a dollar and a half a day." A spokesman for D. J. Devlin had said in 1849 that "the hands are classed (according to their skill, capacity, and promptness) into grades —they earn from $3 up to $15 per week"—and that many were successfully supporting large families.[4] The higher figure undoubtedly included cutters, who drew the leading salaries in the inside shop. According to a report of the New York Chamber of Commerce, cutters in 1857 averaged $13 per week and tailors and pressers averaged $9.

Since the work was seasonal in character, a weekly earning cannot be multiplied by fifty-two to compute a yearly earning. A more correct estimate would be based on an eight-month, or thirty-five-week, working year. On that basis by 1860 cutters earned about $455 a year and tailors and pressers about $310.

Women employed in the inside shop drew lower salaries than did men, although at times they worked alongside the men on identical jobs. In 1861 one manufacturer declared that "the relative wages between men and women are, as sewers, say for men, one-third more." However, the men were generally expected to do the more difficult sewing and such heavy work as sewing overcoats and pressing. The proprietor of a large wholesale house said that he paid women "about $6 per week, men about $9," but that the men did heavier work. Another report indicated that young girls employed in clothing factories in 1858 earned $3 a week.[5] A compilation made by the Massachusetts Bureau of Labor listed these weekly wages for women in 1860: basters, $6.32; operators, $5.53; finishers, $4.56.[6]

One seamstress recalled that when both she and her sister were employed in an inside shop they "were sometimes able to earn eight dollars a week between [them] sometimes only six." At the shirt factory of Winchester and Davis in 1856 "the earnings of the females employed in the ironing rooms [netted] from $3 to $6 per week; and of those engaged in other and subordinate departments, from $3 to $6 per week." The "other and subordinate departments" included buttonhole making which earned about one cent for each buttonhole. And since there were about fourteen buttonholes in each shirt, the seamstresses earned $3 to $4 a week for that task.

Each working day in the inside shop lasted from ten to fourteen hours, and each week included six days. In some factories work was stopped for lunch, but where women worked side by side with men little or no talking was permitted among them.

In the outside shop the statistics are more numerous for the early years of the century, and they show much lower wages than those paid in the inside shop. Indeed, it is precisely because of the meager compensation of the outside workers that literature concerning their wages appeared in such relative abundance. The reformers of the Jacksonian period never seemed to tire of expounding the cause of the poor widowed seamstress.

In 1828 it was said that the most that tailoresses could hope to earn did "not average more than from one dollar to one dollar and a quarter per week."[7] Two years later a New York physician complained that the clothiers were paying "starvation wages." He declared that women were "employed in making duck trowsers for a store not far from Chatham Street, at four cents a pair; and cotton shirts at seven cents a piece." When he inquired as to how much could be produced in a day, he was told that "the utmost which a woman could do, by sitting from morning till night, [was] to sew three pair of pantaloons or one shirt a day." Further, he was told that such rates prevailed throughout the city.[8]

The following decades brought little change in the earnings of the women employed in the outside shop. A report in 1845 showed that the earnings of tailoresses ranged from $1.50 to $2 per week and that "there are very many who cannot, by faithful diligence, earn more than a dollar a week!" Prices paid to tailoresses by wholesale houses that year were as follows:

"Duck trowsers, overalls, etc. eight and ten cents each. Drawers and Undershirts, both flannel and cotton from six to eight cents, at the ordinary shops, and 12½ at the best. One garment is a day's work for some—others can make two.

"Sattinet, cashmere and broadcloath pants sometimes with gaiter buttons and lined, from 18 to 30 cents per pair. One pair is a good days work.

"Vests, 25 to 50 cents–the latter price paid only for work of the very best quality. Good hands make one a day.

"Thin coats are made for 25 to 37½ cents a piece.

"Heavy pilot-cloth coats, with three pockets, $1 each. A cost of this kind cannot be made under three days.

"Cloth roundabouts and pea-jackets, 25 to 50 cents—three can be made in two days."[9]

Shirtmakers received even lower remuneration; the swiftest hands seldom earned more than $1.50 a week.

A survey of the wages paid by fifty New York clothing establishments in 1853 showed that most of the tailoresses employed in sewing men's garments earned only up to twenty-four cents in a twelve-hour working day. The shirtmakers were "paid, numerous instances, at the rate of 8, 7, 5, and some as low as 4 cents a piece, three of them being a hard days labor . . . at the best of the above prices, all doing full work the year round, amounts to *ninety-one dollars!*" Another survey showed that in 1859 the shirtmakers still worked twenty hours a day for a weekly salary of about $3.[10] The owners of sewing machines, however, were able to earn from $3 to $4 a week by 1860, provided that they put in long hours.

The flood of women that rushed to meet the needs of the wholesale clothiers created the opportunity for wages to remain low. Many of the seamstresses were so eager for a chance that they were willing to accept work at any price. In 1828 it was noticed "that on Tuesday last, there were eleven hundred applicants seeking employment . . . in making shirts . . . although it was known none could have more than four, and few more than two per week, at 12½ cents each."[11] Further, with immigrants pouring into New York harbor, and with many of them only too glad to take up the needle for a pittance, a blanket was spread over wages and the less skilled workers of the outside shop were particularly affected. One journal pointed up the problem in 1845 when it declared that "the female population of our city . . . considerably outnumbers the male, while employment . . . is distributed in inverse ratio. There are thus many more seamstresses . . . than are required in that capacity . . . Under these circumstances, nothing can prevent low wages." Moreover, the situation was aggravated by the fact that the outside shop extended far beyond the city and included "competition . . . from the rural sections . . . where rents are nominal, provisions low, and . . . shirts can be made cheaper than in a great city." In fact, throughout the 1840's and 1850's the country tailoresses were accused by contemporaries of being the major cause of the low wages paid in the outside shop.

In all fairness, however, it should be noted that despite the low wages the expanding clothing trade had done some good: it had opened up vast new fields of employment to women. Further, the New York needlewomen were paid higher wages than were the seamstresses in Europe. In fact, some writers actually denied that the women were being exploited at all. One survey of retail and wholesale clothiers in New York in 1856 concluded that "notwithstanding the competition in the trade, and the temptation to lower prices by underpaying labor, the females so employed are comparatively well paid." After examining the books of one wholesaler, the survey disclosed "that women earn from $3 to $7 per week." Even the workingman's friend, the *New-York Daily Tribune,* said in June, 1853, that "many employers . . . refuse to take advantage of the low terms at which labor may be had, and who pays in some instances as much as ten times the price that is allowed at the 'cheap shops.'"

Labor Organizations. In the early years of the nineteenth century the tailors managed to have some say about the prices they received for their labor, but there was little militancy in their demands before 1820, even though a tailors' union existed in the city as early as 1806. In fact, the union's first strike, in 1819, was not so much a demand for increased wages as it was a protest against the employment of women by custom tailors;[12] and that this effort was largely wasted can be seen by the fact that the young tailoresses in New York had organized their own union by 1825 to demand higher wages.[13]

Although the strike was an illegal weapon in early nineteenth century America and strikers were largely doomed to failure and punishment, the tailors did not shy away from such work stoppages. In 1824 tailors struck in Buffalo: they were tried for conspiracy, found guilty, and fined $2 each. Three years later a similar conspiracy trial was held in Philadelphia. In 1833 the New York City tailors participated in their first strike for higher wages. They were organized by the Union Trade Society of Journeymen Tailors, which had been formed the same year. During the strike's duration the tailors requested that societies of tailors throughout the United States prevent their own members from coming to New York. The *New York Journal of Commerce,* however, considered the boycott useless because of the abundance of tailoresses in the city who were only too glad to work for half the price paid to men. And this strike, like those that preceded it, ended in failure.

In October, 1835, the Union Trade Society of Journeymen Tailors once again demanded that prices be increased and called a strike. Since the situation had arisen at the height of the busy season, the clothiers had to consent to the increased rates. The following January, however, when business slowed, the prices were reduced to what they had been formerly. That action set off a strike that was to prove to be the most violent of all strikes up to that time. Both sides were stubborn, refused to give an inch, and resorted to the columns of the newspapers to appeal to public opinion. That March 9 the employers organized the "Society of Master Tailors in the City of New York"; declared the demands of the New York tailors "subversive of the rights of individuals, detrimental to the public good, injurious to business, restrictive of our freedom of action"; and resolved not to "receive into their employ any man who is a member of the Union Trade Society of Journeymen Tailors in the City of New York." The tailors, in turn, picketed the shops of the city, spread their cloaks over the shops' windows to darken their interiors, and insulted and threatened all of the tailors who continued to work. The clothiers then appealed to the police and had a few of the picketing tailors arrested "on a charge of riotous and disorderly conduct, in attacking and abusing their journeymen in their employ." The strike continued its violent course until June,[14] when twenty-five of the leading strikers were tried for combination and conspiracy, found guilty, and heavily fined. Despite its collapse, however, the strike did influence a number of master tailors to comply with the demands of the tailors. To placate public opinion, which had been sharply aroused during the months of strife, two merchants, Holmes and Williams, named their shop at 45 John Street the "Tailors' Union Emporium." In addition, Hoyt and McLeod, Greenwich Street tailors, assured their patrons that "by paying the journeymen's bill of price, they have a decided advantage . . . by having their work well done."[15]

Although 1836 was a milestone in the history of trade unionism in tailoring in New York City, the defeat of the strike did leave considerable discouragement among the ranks of the proponents of militancy. Moreover, the long depression that followed the strike made trade unionism a rather useless weapon. In addition, the rapid rise of the ready-made clothing trade brought into the ranks of labor numerous new elements that would have to be dealt with seriously in future unionism.

The seamstresses and tailoresses were the first in the labor force to feel the pinch of the crisis of 1837. When orders from the South and West came to a halt, thousands were thrown out of work and a "Tailoresses and Seamstresses Benevolent Society" began an appeal for charity. In November, 1836, the society's members called a meeting at the Chatham Street Chapel and invited all "the friends of humanity, to come forward . . . for without your aid we must inevitably suffer in the extreme. Poverty is staring us in the face," they said, "and ere the coming winter closes it is to be feared that many will suffer for the common necessities of life."

Since charity was not enough, however, the tailoresses went into the clothing business themselves the following summer by forming the "Tailoresses' and Seamstresses' Clothing Establishment" at Broadway and Leonard Street. The firm included a custom tailoring department, a children's clothing department, a repair department, an agency that supplied seamstresses to work at the homes of private families, and a wholesale department that filled orders for the South and West. But it did not fulfill its primary purpose—supplying tailoresses and seamstresses with work—because it failed as a business venture and within a few months nothing more was heard of it. "What have become of the Sewing Societies, Assistance Societies, etc.?" the *New York Herald* asked on November 28, 1838. No one seemed to know.

During the following few years little was heard from any organization of tailors, because although a skeleton movement remained, it was largely inactive. With the revival of trade in the early 1840's, however, demands for the improvement of wages were made once more. In the late summer and early fall of 1841 the cutters and clothing store clerks united to demand that all clothing stores in the city close at eight o'clock in the evening. Three summers later the tailors staged another strike against a reduction in wages. During the stoppage 2,000 workers paraded through the principal streets of Manhattan with marching bands.

But it was not until 1850 that the tailors were once again organized in a strong protective society. In fact, they were organized in several societies, because the industry's expansion, its division into custom-made and ready-made factions, and its dearth of immigrant laborers had caused the emergence of a number of groups with varying interests. Thus, there were a Benefit Association of Tailors, a Protective Association of Tailors, an organization of German tailors, a group of English tailors, a society for the workers in custom tailor shops, a union for those employed in the "Southern houses," and several societies for the cutters and clothing clerks.

That year the demand that employers accept a new "bill of prices" brought all of those groups together. Every effort was made to get the city's clothing merchants to agree to the new scale of wages. A strike was called in July and every worker who continued in his job at the old wage was threatened with assault. Late that month a riot broke out on the steps of the Catholic Church on Third Street because the parish priest tried to brave the threats of the strikers by having "two cart loads of un-made garments taken to the Church to be distributed among the tailors of the congregation not engaged in the strike."[16] More positive action was taken in August, when plans were made to open a Tailors' Cooperative Clothing Store through which the German and English protective unions hoped to supply their striking tailors with work at an acceptable level of wages. "The tailors have now the opportunity," the planners announced, "to establish as extensive an establishment as any of those whom they consider their oppressors, and under proper management they are to be successful." The project, however, lacked sufficient financial support from the outset and soon failed.[17]

During the strike the wholesale dealers, too, became active. They intended to halt "the adoption of the list of prices proposed by the journeymen tailors" and on July 25 they called a meeting to consider their plans. All of the merchants agreed that the higher prices would cause them serious harm, since they "could not, at present, obtain a higher profit upon their goods than 20 per cent, which was scarcely sufficient to cover their risks, expenses, etc."[18] Yet, one by one, they were eventually forced to agree to sign the new bill of prices. Only a few were stubborn enough to hold out until the bitter end. When Conant, a member of the firm of Conant and Ball, was approached by a committee of tailors, he roared that "his firm 'will be dammed before they surrender to the journeymen tailors.'" Equally adamant were the firms of Longstreet, Hayes and Snow, and Martin. Nevertheless by August 19 sixty-nine wholesalers had signed the bill of prices. A list of those firms was appended to "The Tailors Appeal," which appeared in the *New-York Daily Tribune.* Part of the appeal stated: "Gentlemen: whereas, a number of the 'Southern' work employers, refuse to give us a fair remuneration for our labor, and as it is utterly impossible for us working for ourselves and families, and as we wish you to fully understand who are the friends of the workingman, we subjoin a list of those employers who have signed our bill of prices, and earnestly call upon you to patronize only those employers who have acted so honorably."[19]

Throughout the remaining years of the decade the tailors continued to meet to discuss wages. Occasionally they also made suggestions for revisions in the bill of prices. In 1853 all of the splinter tailor unions in the city joined forces to form a General Trades Union. Later that year 4,000 tailors went on strike and refused to resume work until their demands were met.[20]

But, although there were a number of strikes—none of which was so violent as the one in 1850—the tailoresses and seamstresses were not included in them; instead, the women were expected to take care of themselves. As a result, they formed their own organizations, such as the American Industrial Union and the Shirt Sewers Union, both of which were established about 1850. The purpose of these organizations was similar to that of the cooperative store—to supply the unemployed seamstresses with work through the formation of a tailoring enterprise—and the capital for the ventures was acquired through donations in the form of dues, which were expected "to pay the expenses of buying the goods and having them cut into garments for the seamstresses to make, for selling the manufactured articles, for rents of hall to meet in and store." In 1853 it was reported that the Shirt Sewers Union had "finally become established, and is at this moment pursuing a prosperous career, giving permanent employment at satisfactory . . . prices to all in its employ."[21] However, the state of prosperity did not continue for long, because the panic of 1857 and the severe depression that followed three years later temporarily halted the union activities and cooperative organizations of both sexes. In fact, by December, 1860, three-fourths of all of the clothing workers in the city were unemployed.

X

MERCHANTS OF DISTINCTION

From the very beginning of the nineteenth century tailors in America were accorded a far more respectable position in society than were tailors in Europe. From the first year of its existence—1786—the Society of Mechanics and Tradesmen of New York City had a custom tailor, Andrew Otterson, on its general committee.[1]

During the early 1800's visitors to this country were surprised at the social role of the tailors in urban and civic affairs. One Englishman, Charles Henry Wilson, was astonished to see a tailor leading a Fourth of July procession in New York in 1819. In a book based upon his personal observation he relates "the singularity of a *Tailor* commanding five thousand men, I consider strange, because the old adage with us is, that for the manufacture of one man, *nine snippies* are requested. . . . Curiosity led me therefore to enquire if such was usual for officers to be mechanics . . . and found it was so."[2] Others commented similarly that the scorn for tailors evident in most European countries did not exist in America.

The fluidity of society in America enabled a number of New York tailors and clothiers who had enjoyed a few successful years in business to drop their needles and enter into real estate, politics, banking, or a comfortable retirement. One story of outstanding success is that of George Opydke, who was born in 1805 in Hunterdon County, New Jersey, and who was one of the first to manufacture ready-made clothing in New York City in 1832. Opdyke moved rapidly from wholesaling clothing to importing dry goods. Later he entered banking, and in 1858 he was elected to the State Assembly as a member of the Republican Party. Two years later he was appointed a delegate to the National Republican Convention in Chicago, and in 1861 he was elected Mayor of New York City, an office he held until 1863. In addition, in 1845 he wrote a scholarly treatise on political economy that was published in 1851. Fifteen years later he published a volume of documents dealing with the political and administrative history of New York City during his mayorality. A comparatively affluent man, in 1850 his personal and real wealth had been valued for taxation at $55,500.[3]

John J. Cisco was another who progressed from dealer in ready-made clothing to political officeholder. One of the city's earliest clothing dealers, he had a shop at 159 Cherry Street in the early 1830's. As a member of the exclusive Knickerbocker Club even in his clothing business days, Cisco associated with New York's finest folk. In 1850, when he became assistant subtreasurer of the city, his real and personal property were valued for taxation at $43,500.[4]

Another clothier was Robert Jones, who was reputed to be worth $250,000 in 1845. Active as a Whig, he was eventually elected alderman of the fifth ward.[5] Still another clothier—and an alderman of the second ward—was Samuel St. John. Reputed to be worth $300,000 in 1845, he acknowledged that most of his money had been made "by fortunate investments in real estate, and by loaning during pressures."[6]

The Seligmans, a family of clothiers, achieved even more success as bankers after the outbreak of the Civil War than they had achieved as manufacturers and wholesalers of ready-made clothing before the conflict. The family ultimately opened branches of its banks in London, Paris, and Frankfurt, and because of its international connections it proved helpful in floating Union government bonds in European markets.

A student of merchandising and a clothier with thirty years of experience, Samuel H. Terry wrote at the close of his career in 1869 that "few are there among all who have been in business, that have accumulated at fifty years of age $45,000, or will be worth at sixty years of age . . . $100,000."[7] A survey of men in the clothing business, however, showed that by the 1850's there were more than a few who had accumulated even larger amounts.

James Chesterman, who arrived in New York "poor" in the early nineteenth century and opened a tailor shop at John and Nassau Streets, prospered by adding the importation of ready-made clothing to his tailoring business. By 1845 his wealth was estimated at $300,000, and ten years later, when his estate was divided, it was valued at $1,000,000.[8] Abner Weyman, who in 1810 was manufacturing ready-made clothing "suitable for sea, the country, or southern trade," was listed in a survey of the city's rich men in 1845 as "one of the richest 'tailors' of our City." His wealth that year was estimated at $200,000. One of his relatives, Edmund H. Weyman, who was also in the clothing business, had a personal fortune of $150,000 in 1855.[9]

James Scofield, another of New York's successful clothiers, had his personal wealth computed at $150,000 in 1845. That year Moses Yale Beach's survey of the city's wealthy men described him as "a very industrious and worthy tailor, who, from a poor boy became a rich man, and the head of the celebrated firm of Scofield, Phelps & Co., which house has been for the last thirty-five years the largest and most fashionable tailoring establishment in the City."[10] His son, William Scofield, who managed the business and served as chief cutter, possessed an estate of $250,000.

Richard Mortimer, who operated a tailor shop in the city for many years, retired to "a large estate" in the early 1840's. And his wealth, which was estimated in 1845 at $400,000, was only part of his good fortune: his daughter, famed for her beauty, "was deemed beyond all question, the reigning belle at Saratoga." Sylvanus B. Stilwell did not enter the clothing business until 1840, when he went into partnership with Montross of New Orleans. But success came quickly, because by 1855 his personal wealth was figured at $175,000. Abel T. Edgerton, who arrived in New York from New Haven about 1820 and opened a clothing store on Fulton Street, was worth $100,000 by 1845. However, part of that—$25,000—had come from a successful marriage in 1841 to "a niece of John Hardenbrook." Edward S. Brooks and Elisa Brooks of the Brooks Brothers firm were each worth $250,000 by 1855. Unlike the other merchants, who had transferred their wealth into various investments, they were said to have made their fortunes largely at the clothing establishment, which their father had founded in 1818.[11]

There were also many merchants by the end of the 1850's who had not amassed fortunes in the hundreds of thousands of dollars, but who had, nevertheless, achieved comfortable material existences. William H. Boyd's list of the persons and copartnerships taxed in 1856 and 1857 shows that, according to the assessor's books of that fiscal year—and since this is an estimate for taxation, it must be considered a minimum estimate—22 clothiers claimed a real and personal property evaluation at between $5,000 and $10,000. In addition, 9 were between $10,001 and $15,000, 6 between $15,001 and $20,000, 4 between $20,001 and $25,000, 1 between $25,001 and $30,000, 3 between $30,001 and $35,000, 2 between $35,001 and $40,000, 1 between $40,001 and $45,000, 4 between $50,001 and $55,000, 1 between $75,001 and $80,000, 1 between $80,001 and $85,000, and 1 between $95,001 and $100,000.[12]

New York's tailors and tailoresses, too, were probably well off as a group by the end of the 1850's. According to statements of the Bowery, Manhattan, Greenwich, Bleecker, Emigrant, Industrial, and Irving savings banks in 1857, the clothiers, tailors, tailoresses, and seamstresses constituted the leading group of depositors. In fact, the tailors and seamstresses alone as depositors numbered 2,404; and, as one of 232 occupational and professional groups surveyed by those savings institutions, they were surpassed by only the domestic workers.

XI

OVERVIEW

The New York clothing trade had expanded to the point of national pre-eminence by 1861 largely because it was in a better position than was the industry in any other urban area in the country to supply the growing demand for clothing. Moreover, it was located so well geographically and commercially that all streams of traffic converged at its doorstep. Both raw materials and an abundant labor force poured into it from the Old World, and the unindustrialized and underdeveloped areas of the New World—the South and West—looked to it for a steady supply of clothing.

New York's merchants took every advantage of their city's commercial supremacy. They intensified the market's attractiveness in every conceivable way and concentrated their efforts in luring the country buyers with abundant advertising, attractive credit policies, well-regulated auctions, huge displays, vigorous promotions of fashionable ready-made and custom-made garments, and an immense variety of merchandise. Further, the merchants took advantage of the great need for clothing in the unindustrialized areas of the United States by establishing sales outlets in, and sending representatives to, New Orleans, Charleston, Savannah, St. Louis, Chicago, San Francisco, and other cities.

No location in America seemed beyond the reach of the New York merchants, who shipped their invoices all around with clock-like regularity.

In addition, the New York clothing industry fed upon the city's own growing population. Every convenience was offered to the retail buyer just as it was to the wholesale buyer, and the merchants stimulated local trade by frequently advertising prices and custom-made and ready-made fashions in newspapers, on huge placards and signs, and by means of hard-hitting salesmanship and other traffic-stopping devices.

The productive machinery of the New York clothiers met every test imposed on it by the increasing national demand. Both the custom tailor shops and the wholesale plants adopted systematized management, and mechanization and technology became the bywords of all operations.

By 1861 the New York clothing trade had emerged as one of the outstanding factors in the city's economic life. It had given fortunes to a few and employment to thousands. Its advantages had been shared by women as well as men. And the few crises that befell it—from 1837 to 1842, from 1857 to 1858, and from 1860 to 1861—did not hamper its long-range growth. When the Civil War broke out the New York clothing dealers were immediately able to alter their production from that of ready-made garments for men to that of uniforms for the Union troops. But that is another story.

REFERENCES

CHAPTER I

1. U.S. Department of Commerce, *The Men's Factory-Made Clothing Industry* (Washington, 1916), p. 9; Albert S. Bolles, *Industrial History of the United States* (Norwich, Connecticut, 1879), p. 399.

2. Amanda Jones, *The Tailor's Assistant for Cutting Men's Clothes by the Square Rule* (Whitehall Vermont, 1823), p. 3.

3. Isaac Holmes, *An Account of the United States of America Derived from Actual Observation* (London, 1823), p. 125.

4. Entry (in pounds and shillings) of June 18, 1818, Day Book of Henry S. Brooks, Brooks Brothers, Inc., New York.

CHAPTER II

1. Holmes, pp. 127-28.

2. John F. Jones, *Jones's New York Mercantile and General Directory* (New York, 1806), pp. 110 ff.

3. David Longworth, *Longworth's American Almanack, New York Register,* (New York, 1805), pp. 160-62. (This work will hereafter be cited as *Longworth's Directory.*)

4. Advertisement of Kirtland, Bronson, and Co. in *Harper's Weekly,* viii (Feb., 1864), 141; Freeman Hunt, ed., *The Merchants' Magazine and Commercial Review,* L (March, 1864), 233. (This work will hereafter be cited as *Hunt's Merchants' Magazine.*)

5. *Annual Report of the Chamber of Commerce of the State of New York, for the Year 1858* (New York, 1859), p. 38.

6. Edwin Williams, *The New-York Annual Register for the Year of Our Lord 1836* (New York, 1836), pp. 360, 504.

7. *Eighth Census of the United States,* 1860, *Manufactures,* p. LXIV.

8. Edwin T. Freedley, ed., *Leading Pursuits and Leading Men* (Philadelphia, 1856), p. 125.

9. *Hunt's Merchants' Magazine,* XX (March, 1849), 348; *Andrews Co.'s Stranger's Guide in the City of New York* (New York, 1849), p. 24.

10. Adna F. Weber, *The Growth of Industry in New York.* New York State Department of Labor, (Albany, 1904), pp. 34-5.

11. *Seventh Census of the United States,* 1850, pp. LXIX, LXXVII.

12. Charles R. Rode, *Rode's New York Business Directory, 1853-1854* (New York, 1855), pp. 37 ff.

13. H. M. Wilson, *Wilson's Business Directory of New York City, 1854-1855* (New York, 1855), pp. 37 ff.

14. *Census of the State of New York for 1855* (Albany, 1857), pp. 192-93, 406.

15. *Fourth Annual Report of the Chamber of Commerce of the State of New York, for the Year 1861-62* (New York, 1862), p. 204.

16. *The Mirror of Fashion* (Dec. 1854), p. 154.

17. Boston Board of Trade, *Second Annual Report of the Government* (Boston, 1856), p. 45.

18. D. Morier Evans, *The History of the Commercial Crisis, 1857-58, and the Stock Exchange Panic of 1859.* (London, 1859), p. 126.

19. *New York Daily Tribune,* Sept. 23, 1858; *New York Herald,* Aug. 29, Sept. 20, 1858; June 13, 1859.

20. *Eighth Census of the United States,* 1860, *Manufactures,* p. LX.

21. *Ibid.,* pp. 252, 380, 413, 523, 539. (Figures of the U.S. census are useful mainly as a basis of comparing the production of the various states. Their accuracy is, however, doubtful, because the city directories show that many firms were not counted by the census officials. Moreover, the estimate of the value of the product does not agree with the annual report of the New York Chamber of Commerce of that year.)

22. *Report of the Secretary of the Treasury of the Commerce and Navigation of the United States* (Washington, 1856-1860), 1855-1860.

CHAPTER III

1. Bayard Still, *Mirror for Gotham; New York as Seen by Contemporaries from Dutch Days to the Present* (New York, 1956), p. 55; Fred M. Jones, *Middlemen in the Domestic Trade of the United States, 1800-1860* (Urbana, Illinois, 1937), pp. 16-17.

2. Francis Wysc, *America, Its Realities and Resources* (London, 1846), II, 371-72.

3. Wyse, II, 373.

4. *Ibid.,* March 12, 1839.

5. *News Orleans Daily Picayune,* July 28, 1848.

6. *Savannah Georgian,* Aug. 18, 1831.

7. *New Orleans Daily Picayune,* Feb. 23, 1851.

8. *Longworth's Directory,* 1824-1825, p. 6; *New York Journal of Commerce,* Oct. 3, 4, 1834; *New York Herald,* Feb. 18, 1836.

9. *Ibid.,* July 29, 1837.

10. Isabella L. B. Bishop, *The Englishwoman in America* (London, 1856), p. 342.

11. Wyse, II, 375-77; John B. Jones, *Life and Adventures of a Country Merchant* (Philadelphia, 1854), pp. 266-72.

12. "Clothier Advertising in 1850," *Bulletin of the Business Historical Society,* VII, No. 6 (Dec. 1933), 11.

13. *Hunt's Merchants' Magazine,* XXXVI (Jan. 1857), 134.

14. Roy A. Foulke, *The Sinews of American Commerce* (New York, 1941), pp. 68-9, 156.

15. Francis J. Grund, *The Americans in Their Moral, Social, and Political Relations* (London, 1837), I, 108, 166; Benjamin F. Foster, *The Merchant's Manual, Comprising the Principles of Trade, Commerce and Banking* (Boston, 1838), pp. 47-8.

16. *Savannah Georgian,* Aug. 18, 1831.

17. Boston Board of Trade, *Third Annual Report of the Government . . . 1856,* p. 63; *Fourth Annual Report . . . 1858,* p. 83.

18. Samuel H. Terry, *The Retailer's Manual: Embodying the Conclusions of Thirty Years' Experience in Merchandising* (Newark, New Jersey, 1869), p. 91; Benjamin F. Foster, *The Clerks' Guide, or Commercial Correspondence; Comprising Letters of Business, Forms of Bills, Invoices, Account-Sales . . .* (Boston, 1837), p. 43.

19. Fisher, Blashfield and Co., Merchants, New York, N. Y., 1845-1865, Credit Ratings, New York Public Library.

20. Robert G. Albion, *The Rise of the New York Port, 1815-1860* (New York, 1939), p. 38.

21. Moses Y. Beach, *Wealth and Wealthy Citizens of New York City* (New York, 1842), 2nd edition, p. 3; 1855, 12th edition, p. 18.

22. Edward S. Abdy, *Journal of a Residence and Tour in the United States of North America from April, 1833, to October, 1834* (London, 1835), I, 296-97.

23. *Report of the Secretary of the Treasury of the Commerce and Navigation of the United States, 1855-1860.*

24. Herbert Heaton, "Benjamin Gott and the Anglo-American Cloth Trade," *Journal of Economic and Business History,* II (Nov., 1929), 147.

25. C. D. Arfwedson, *The United States and Canada in 1832, 1833 and 1834* (London, 1834), I, 230; Terry, pp. 307-08.

26. Ray B. Westerfield, "Early History of American Auctions—A Chapter in Commercial History," *Transactions of the Connecticut Academy of Arts and Sciences,* XXIII (May, 1920), 196.

27. *New York Commercial Advertiser,* Jan. 21, 1801; *New York Evening Post,* April 21, Oct. 31, 1812; Jan. 18, Aug. 9, 1815; Heaton, p. 149; *Mirror of Fashion* (July, 1854), p. 120; (Dec. 1854), p. 160; *New York Herald,* Sept. 12, 1853.

28. *New York American Citizen,* Jan. 28, 1807.

29. Contracts, dated Sept. 17, 1823, and Feb. 10, 1827, between John H. Browning and C. A. Whitman, New York Public Library.

30. *New York Herald,* April 21, 1843; *New Orleans Daily Picayune,* June 3, 1851; Isaac Markens, *The Hebrews in America* (New York, 1888), p. 142.

31. *Eighth Census of the United States,* 1860, *Manufactures,* p. LXIV.

32. Wyse, II, 383.

33. Edmund M. Blunt, *The Picture of New York and Stranger's Guide to the Commercial Metropolis of the United States* (New York, 1828), pp. 452-55.

34. Westerfield, pp. 181-82, 196-97.

35. *New York Evening Post,* Feb. 1, June 6, 1833.

36. *New York Herald,* June 28, 1861.

37. Virginia Penny, *The Employments of Women: A Cyclopedia of Woman's Work* (Boston, 1863), p. 135.

38. Jesse E. Pope, *The Clothing Industry in New York* (Columbia, Missouri, 1905), pp. 6-7.

39. William M. Bobo, *Glimpses of New York City by a South Carolinian Who Had Nothing Else To Do* (Charleston, 1852), pp. 115, 117.

40. George G. Foster, *New York in Slices: By an Experienced Carver* (New York, 1849), p. 14.

41. U.S. Department of Commerce, *The Men's Factory-Made Clothing Industry,* pp. 9-10.

42. *New York Herald,* Oct. 10, 1840.

43. *Hunt's Merchants' Magazine,* XX (Jan., 1849), p. 116; Freedley, *Leading Pursuits,* pp. 130-31.
44. *Ibid.,* pp. 133-34.
45. Brooks Brothers, Inc., *Brooks Brothers Centenary,* 1818-1918 (New York, 1918), pp. 11-2, 18, 22, 25; *Andrews & Co.'s Stranger's Guide,* p. 25.
46. Freedley, *Leading Pursuits,* pp. 132-33.
47. Chauncey M. Depew, ed., *One Hundred Years of American Commerce* (New York, 1895), II, 561.
48. *Ibid.,* II, 565; Freedley, *Leading Pursuits,* pp. 141-42, 144.
49. *Ibid.,* pp. 135-41; *Hunt's Merchants' Magazine,* XX (March, 1849), 348.

CHAPTER IV

1. Advertisement of Kirtland, Bronson, and Co. in *Harper's Weekly,* VIII (Feb. 1864), 141.
2. *New York Herald,* Aug. 25, 1836.
3. Philip S. Foner, *Business and Slavery: The New York Merchants and the Irrespressible Conflict* (Chapel Hill, North Carolina, 1941), p. 1.
4. *Charleston Courier,* Sept. 29, 1825; *Columbus Enquirer,* July 5, 1834.
5. Williams, pp. 340-41.
6. *New Orleans Daily Picayune,* Sept. 25, 1846.
7. Charles H. Wesley, *Negro Labor in the U.S.* (New York, 1927), pp. 34, 38, 44.
8. Quoted in Atherton, *Southern Country Store,* pp. 141-42.
9. John P. Campbell, *Nashville Business Directory,* (Nashville, 1857), p. 161.
10. Freedley, *Leading Pursuits,* p. 138.
11. *New York Herald,* Aug. 1, 1860.
12. Harold Sinclair, *The Port of New Orleans* (New York, 1942), p. 169.
13. John A. Paxton, *The New Orleans Directory and Register* (New Orleans, 1822), p. 3; Atlanta, *Southern Miscellany, and Upper Georgia Whig,* Dec. 4, 1847.
14. Data derived from local directories.
15. James Stuart, *Three Years in North America* (London, 1833), I, 523.
16. George Wilson, *Portrait Gallery of the Chamber of Commerce of the State of New York* (New York, 1890), pp. 61-2.
17. *New Orleans Daily Picayune,* May 22, 1847.
18. Freedley, *Leading Pursuits,* p. 135; *New Orleans Daily Picayune,* Feb. 2, 1853.
19. *New York Daily Tribune,* Sept. 23, 1858; *New York Herald,* Dec. 20, 1860.
20. *Hunt's Merchants' Magazine,* XX (March, 1849), 348.
21. Beach, *The Wealth and Biography of the Wealthy Citizens of the City of New York,* 1855, p. 69.
22. *New Orleans Daily Picayune,* Nov. 15, 1843.
23. *Ibid.,* Oct. 14, 1852.
24. *Ibid.,* June 16, 1847; July 17, 1851.
25. *Ibid.,* Feb. 4, 1857.
26. H. and A. Cohen, *Cohen's New Orleans Directory* (New Orleans, 1854), pp. 255, 259-60, 267-68.
27. *New Orleans Daily Picayune,* Oct. 16, 1847.
28. *Ibid.,* Jan. 15, 1851.
29. Kenneth M. Stampp, *The Peculiar Institution: Slavery in the Ante-Bellum South* (New York, 1956), pp. 289-92.

30. James D. B. DeBow, *The Industrial Resources, etc., of the Southern and Western States* (New Orleans, 1852-53), II, 331-34, 336.
31. John R. McCulloch, *A Dictionary of Commerce and Commercial Navigation* (Philadelphia, 1840-41), II, 30, 34, 795.
32. *Macon Telegraph,* Nov. 21, 1826; *New York Herald,* June 22, 1836.
33. Foner, pp. 159-61.
34. William H. Russell, *My Dairy North and South* (New York, 1954), pp. 185-86.
35. *New York Herald,* June 3, 1861.
36. *Ibid.,* Nov. 27, 1860.
37. *Ibid.,* Nov. 27, 1860.
38. *New Orleans Daily Picayune,* Nov. 25, 1860; Jan. 13, 1861.

CHAPTER V

1. Emory R. Johnson, T. W. Van Metre, and others, *History of Domestic and Foreign Commerce of the United States* (Washington, 1915), I, 237-38.
2. Balthaser H. Meyer and C. E. MacGill, *History of Transportation in the United States Before 1860* (Washington, 1917), pp. 86, 93, 168.
3. Thomas J. Scharf, *History of Saint Louis City and County* (Philadelphia, 1883), II, 1037.
4. *New York Journal of Commerce,* March 2, 1834.
5. *St. Louis Liberia Advocate,* September, 1849.
6. James Hall, *The West: Its Commerce and Navigation* (Cincinnati, 1848), p. 246.
7. John Moses and Joseph Kirkland, *History of Chicago, Illinois* (Chicago, 1895), I, 294-95.
8. George S. Hellman, "Joseph Seligman, American Jew," *Publications of the American Jewish Historical Society,* XLI (Sept., 1951), 31.
9. J. N. Taylor and M. O. Crooks, *Sketch Book of Saint Louis* (St. Louis, 1858), pp. 239 ff.
10. Boston Board of Trade, *Fourth Annual Report . . . 1858,* p. 84.
11. Charles Cist, *Sketches and Statistics of Cincinnati in 1859,* (Cincinnati, 1859), pp. 271 ff.
12. Richard Edwards and M. Hopewell, *Edwards' Great West and Her Commercial Metropolis* (St. Louis, 1860), p. 365.
13. Chambers and Knapp, *The St. Louis Directory for the Years 1854-5* (St. Louis, 1854), pp. 220, 226, 237-38.
14. Taylor and Crooks, pp. 325, 341-43.
15. *Hunt's Merchants' Magazine,* XXXII (June, 1855), 693.

CHAPTER VI

1. Allan Nevins, ed., *The Diary of Philip Hone, 1828-1851* (New York, 1927), II, 858.
2. Frank Soulé, John H. Gihon, and James Nisbet, *The Annals of San Francisco* (New York, 1854), pp. 214, 253.

3. H. Hamlin, "Levi Strauss—California Pioneer," *The Pony Express,* XVII Dec. 1950), 1.

4. *New York Herald,* Jan. 22, March 21, 1849; Feb. 5, 1851; *New York Daily Tribune,* Jan 15, 1850.

5. Wheaton J. Lane, *Commodore Vanderbilt* (New York, 1942), pp. 85-91, 93-4, 96-7, 111.

6. Albert M. Friedenberg, ed. "Letters of a California Pioneer," *Publications of the American Jewish Historical Society,* No. 31 (1928), pp. 150-51, 169-70.

7. *San Francisco Daily Alta California,* May 7, 1851.

8. *Annual Report of the Chamber of Commerce of the State of New-York . . . 1859-60,* p. 284.

9. Felix Reisenberg, Jr., *Golden Gate; The Story of San Francisco Harbor* (New York, 1940), p. 64.

10. *San Francisco Daily Alta California,* Oct. 2, 1851.

11. Soulé, pp. 459-60; *Hunt's Merchants' Magazine,* XXIX (July, 1853), 131.

12. Henry G. Langley, *The San Francisco Directory for the Year 1858* (San Francisco, 1858), pp. 309, 325.

13. Boner, pp. 1-15.

14. *San Francisco Daily Alta California,* Feb. 12, Dec. 4, 1852.

15. *San Francisco Daily Alta California,* Dec. 4, 1852.

16. Friedenberg, pp. 143, 145, 155, 166.

17. Alonzo Phelps, *Contemporary Biography of California's Representative Men* (San Francisco, 1881), pp. 330-31.

18. Earl Ramey, *The Beginnings of Marysville* (San Francisco, 1936), pp. 1, 95, 105.

19. Bert H. Olson, "Levi Strauss Western Pioneer Manufacturer," *The Quarterly Historical Society of Southern California,* XXX (Sept. 1948), 209-12.

20. *Ibid.,* May 18, 1852.

21. Phelps, pp. 75-6

22. Soulé, pp. 598-600, 603, 611, 613; *San Francisco Daily Alta California,* May 7, 1851.

23. Friedenberg, pp. 144, 150, 157-58.

CHAPTER VII

1. Albion, p. 142.

2. Stuart, II, 496.

3. Edgar W. Martin, *The Standard of Living in 1860* (Chicago, 1942), pp. 199-200.

4. *Baton Rouge Democratic Advocate,* May 28, 1845.

5. John Fowler, *Journal of a Tour in the State of New York in the Year 1830* (London, 1831), p. 232.

6. *Hunt's Merchants' Magazine,* XXXI (July, 1854), 138.

7. *The Mirror of Fashion* (Nov., 1853), p. 26.

8. Kenneth Dameron, *Men's Wear Merchandising* (New York, 1930), pp. 73-80; Elisabeth McClellan, *Historic Dress in America, 1800-1870* (Philadelphia, 1910), pp. 347 ff.

9. Emmeline S. Wortley, *Travels in the United States, etc., During 1849 and 1850* (London, 1851), I, 287.

10. *New York Herald,* Oct. 14, 1851.
11. *New York American Citizen,* Nov. 8, 1808; *New York Evening Post,* Oct. 30, 1807; June 16, 1820.
12. *New York American Citizen,* Feb. 9, 1809; *New York Evening Post,* Oct. 21, 1822.
13. *New York Atlas or Literary, Historical and Commercial Reporter,* June 20, 1829; *New York Evening Post,* July 2, 1834.
14. *The Mirror of Fashion,* 1853-1855.
15. *Ibid.* (Oct., 1855), p. 81.
16. Charles J. Stowell, *The Journeymen Tailors' Union of America* (Urbana, Illinois, 1918), p. 20.
17. Carl Bridenbaugh, *The Colonial Craftsman* (New York, 1950), p. 70.
18. Charles H. Haswell, *Reminiscences of an Octogenarian of the City of New York* (New York, 1897), pp. 76-7.
19. John B. Jones, *The Western Merchant* (Philadelphia, 1849), p. 185.
20. Jacob Reed's Sons, "The Story of 125 Years of Public Confidence," *Stores* (May, 1949), p. 23.
21. Stephen N. Winslow, *Biographies of Successful Philadelphia Merchants* (Philadelphia, 1864), p. 91.
22. E. Moses and Son, *The Growth of an Important Branch of British Industry* (London, 1860), p. 4.
23. Henry Wampen, *Mathematical Instruction in Constructing Models for Draping the Human Figure* (London, 1863), pp. 14-5.
24. "Human Clothing, Dyeing, and Calico Printing," *The United States Magazine and Democratic Review,* XIX (Oct., 1846), 305.
25. *New York Herald,* June 4, 1838; Feb. 22, 1843; Aug. 14, 1845.
26. Winslow, pp. 92-3.
27. Wilson's Business Directory of 1856-57, p. 60; Trow, *Business Directory . . . 1862-63,* pp. 54, 489.
28. Data from Brooks Brothers, Inc.
29. *New York Herald,* Sept. 23, 1840.
30. Carl H. Juergens, "Movement of Wholesale Prices in New York, 1825-1863," *Publications of the American Statistical Association,* XII (1912), 546.
31. This table is based upon 50 advertisements appearing in the *New York Herald,* 1838-1844.
32. This data is based upon advertisements appearing in *Ibid.,* 1838-1844.
33. This data is based upon advertisements appearing in *Ibid.,* 1845-1860.
34. William Brooks, Day Book, 1835-1837.
35. Fowler, p. 232; Calvin Colton, *Manual for Emigrants to America* (London, 1832), p. 199.
36. *New York Herald,* May 14, 1844.
37. William Chambers, *Things as They Are in America* (London, 1857), p. 190.
38. Brooks Brothers, Inc., *Centenary,* p. 9.
39. Thomas H. James, *Rambles in the United States* (London, 1846), p. 58.
40. Bobo, pp. 161-62.
41. James D. Burn, *Three Years Among the Working-Classes in the United States During the War* (London, 1865), p. 120.
42. Terry, p. 123.
43. *New York Herald,* Oct. 1, 1838.

44. Brooks Brothers, Inc, *Centenary,* p. 21.
45. *New York Herald,* Dec. 16, 1854.
46. Frederick Marryat, *A Diary in America* (New York, 1839), pp. 21-2.
47. Fearon, pp. 10-11.
48. Thomas Hamilton, *Men and Manners in America* (Philadelphia, 1833), p. 24.
49. Ralph M. Hower, "Urban Retailing 100 Years Ago," *Bulletin of the Business Historical Society,* XII (Dec., 1938), 93.
50. *New York Herald,* July 19, 1853.
51. Bishop, p. 340.
52. Fitz-Hugh Ludlow, "The American Metropolis," *The Atlantic Monthly,* XV (Jan. 1865), 85.
53. Terry, pp. 115-16.
54. Peter Neilson, *Recollections of a Six Years' Residence in the United States of America* (Glasgow, 1830), p. 34.
55. Still, p. 155; Bishop, p. 340.
56. *Hunt's Merchants' Magazine,* XX (Jan. 1849), p. 119.

CHAPTER VIII

1. Charles E. Zaretz, *The Amalgamated Clothing Workers of America* (New
2. William H. Stinemets, *A Complete and Permanent System of Cutting All Kinds of Garments to Fit the Human Form on a New and Scientific Principle* (New York, 1843), p. 56.
3. Harvey L. Eades, *The Tailor's Division System* (Union Village, Ohio, 1849), p. 1.
4. W. E. Walker, *The Tailor's Philosophy* (London, 1850), pp. 7-9, 12-14; Eades, p. 1.
5. *New York Evening Post,* Sept. 7, 1830.
6. Scott and Perkins, *The Tailor's Master-Piece* (New York, 1837), pp. 2-3.
7. *New York Herald,* Aug. 2, 1844.
8. Williams, p. 360.
9. *New York Herald,* May 19, 1836.
10. *Annual Report of the Chamber of Commerce of the State of New York,* 1858, p. 38.
11. Wilbur W. S. Shepperson, *British Emigration to North America* (London, 1957), p. 18.
12. *Hunt's Merchants' Magazine,* L (March, 1864), 235; Robert Ernst, *Immigrant Life in New York City, 1825-1863* (New York, 1949), pp. 92, 215, 217.
13. *Eighth Census of the United States,* 1860, *Manufactures,* p. LXIV; Freedley, *Leading Pursuits,* p. 127.
14. *Census of the State of New York for 1855,* p. 406.
15. Freedley, *Philadelphia and Its Manufactures,* pp. 221-22.
16. *Hunt's Merchants' Magazine,* XX (March, 1849), 348.
17. *New York Herald,* July 7, 1848; July 12, 1854.
18. Beach, *Wealth and Biography,* fifth edition, 1845, p. 26.
19. *Eighth Census of the United States,* 1860, *Manufactures,* p. LXV.
20. *Annual Reports of the Quartermaster-General from 1861 to 1866* (Washington, 1880), 1865, p. 11.
21. *New York Herald,* July 26, 1860.

22. *Ibid.*, March 12, 1860.
23. Bell, p. 233; Penny, p. 144.
24. Penny, p. 11; *New York Herald,* Sept. 2, 1855; Pope, p. 29.
25. Freedley, *Leading Pursuits,* p. 141.
26. *New York Herald,* Jan. 28, 1856.
27. *Hunt's Merchants' Magazine,* XXVIII (Aug. 1853), 524.
28. [Anon.] "Needle and Garden. The Story of a Seamstress Who Laid Down Her Needle and Became a Strawberry Girl." *Atlantic Monthly,* XV (April, 1865), 466.
29. *Ibid.*, pp. 153-54.
30. Freedley, *Philadelphia and Its Manufactures,* pp. 223-24.
31. Department of Commerce, *The Shirt and Collar Industries* (Washington, 1916), p. 8.
32. Stuart, I, 522-23; Edith Abbott, *Women in Industry* (New York, 1910), p. 240.
33. *New York Daily Tribune,* Aug. 14, 1845; Penny, p. 114.
34. *Hunt's Merchants' Magazine* XX (Jan. 1849), 116.
35. *New York Herald,* Jan. 5, 1847.
36. Penny, p. 114.
37. "Needle and Garden," *Atlantic Monthly* XV (Feb. 1865), 169.
38. Pope, pp. 41-2; Penny, pp. 112-14.
39. *New-York Daily Tribune,* June 8, 1853.
40. Frederick L. Lewton, "The Servant in the House: A Brief History of the Sewing Machine," *Annual Report of the Board of Regents of the Smithsonian Institution* (Washington, 1930), pp. 560-65.
41. Leander J. Bishop, *A History of American Manufactures* (Philadelphia, 1868), II, 491.
42. Depew, II, 533-34.
43. Lewton, pp. 573-75.
44. *New York Working Man's Advocate,* April 3, 1830.
45. *New-York Daily Tribune,* June 18, 1853.
46. "Needle and Garden," *Atlantic Monthly,* XV (Feb., 1865), 173-76.
47. William E. Baxter, *America and the Americans* (London, 1855), p. 109.
48. Edwin T. Freedley, *Opportunities for Industry and the Safe Investment of Capital; or a Thousand Chances to Make Money* (Philadelphia, 1859) pp. 345-55.
49. Waldemar Kaempffert, ed., *A Popular History of American Inventions* (New York, 1924), II, 389.
50. "Needle and Garden," *Atlantic Monthly,* XV (Feb. 1865), p. 117; (March, 1865), p. 320.
51. *Hunt's Merchants' Magazine,* XXXXI (Dec. 1859), 755; *New York Herald,* Nov. 16, 1858.
52. Cist, p. 363.
53. "Needle and Garden," *Atlantic Monthly,* XV (Feb. 1865), 175-76.

CHAPTER IX

1. *New-York Daily Tribune,* July 18, 1850.
2. U.S. Department of Labor, *History of Wages,* p. 113.
3. *New-York Daily Tribune,* Aug. 19, 1850.

4. Alexander Marjoribanks, *Travels in South and North America* (London, 1853), p. 456.

5. *Annual Report of the Chamber of Commerce of the State of New York . . . 1858*, p. 38.

6. Pope, p. 33.

7. Matthew Carey, *Miscellaneous Essays* (Philadelphia, 1830), p. 174.

8. *New York Working Man's Advocate,* Sept. 11, 1830.

9. *New-York Daily Tribune,* March 7, Aug. 14, 1845.

10. *Hunt's Merchants' Magazine,* XXXXII (June, 1850), 750.

11. Carey, p. 159.

12. Charles J. Stowell, *Studies in Trade Unionism in the Custom Tailoring Trade* (Bloomington, Illinois, 1912), p. 43.

13. *Ibid.*, p. 44.

14. John R. Commons and others, *History of Labour in the United States* (New York, 1918-1935), I, 408; *New York Herald,* Feb. 18, 1836.

15. Commons, V, 315-22; *New York Herald,* April 12, May 3, 1836.

16. *New-York Daily Tribune,* July 19, 25, 29, Aug. 19, 1850; *New York Herald,* July 31, 1850.

17. *New-York Daily Tribune,* Aug. 12, 13, 1850.

18. *Ibid.*, July 26, 1850.

19. *Ibid.*, Aug. 19, 1850.

20. *New York Herald,* Sept. 10, 1851.

21. *New-York Daily Tribune,* July 1, 1850; June 8, 1853.

CHAPTER X

1. Thomas Earle and Charles T. Congdon, ed., *Annals of the General Society of Mechanics and Tradesmen in New York, 1785-1880* (New York, 1882), p. 10.

2. Charles H. Wilson, *The Wanderer in America* (Thirsk, Quebec, 1821), pp. 28-30.

3. William A. Darling, *List of Persons, Copartnerships, and Corporations, Who Were Taxed on Seventeen Thousand Five Hundred Dollars, and Upwards, in the City of New York, in the Year 1850* (New York, 1851), p. 67.

4. Joseph A. Scoville, *The Old Merchants of New York City* (New York, 1862-1866), II, 362-63.

5. Beach, fifth edition, 1845, p. 17.

6. *Ibid.*, fifth edition, 1845, p. 28.

7. Terry, p. 336.

8. Albion, p. 64; Beach, sixth edition, 1845, p. 64; twelfth edition, 1855, p. 18.

9. *New York Evening Post,* Jan. 24, 1810; Beach, fifth edition, 1845, p. 31; twelfth edition, 1855, p. 79.

10. *Ibid.*, fifth edition, 1845, p. 26.

11. *Ibid.*, fifth edition, 1945, pp. 11-12.

12. William H. Boyd, *Boyd's New York City Tax-Book* (New York, 1857), pp. 3 ff; *Wilson's Business Directory of 1857* was used to determine which persons listed in Boyd's volume were active in the clothing business.

13. *New York Herald,* Oct. 31, 1857.

INDEX